Larry Belling

Stroke of Luck

BLOOMSBURY

Bloomsbury Methuen Drama
An imprint of Bloomsbury Publishing Plc

50 Bedford Square	1385 Broadway
London	New York
WC1B 3DP	NY 10018
UK	USA

www.bloomsbury.com

Bloomsbury is a registered trade mark of Bloomsbury Publishing Plc

First published 2014

© Belling Productions Inc. 2014

Lawrence N. Belling has asserted his right under the Copyright, Designs and Patents Act, 1988, to be identified as author of this work.

British Library Cataloguing-in-Publication Data
A catalogue record for this book is available from the British Library.

ISBN: PB: 978-1-4725-7321-6
ePub: 978-1-4725-7323-0
ePDF: 978-1-4725-7322-3

Library of Congress Cataloging-in-Publication Data
A catalog record for this book is available from the Library of Congress.

Typeset by Mark Heslington Ltd, Scarborough, North Yorkshire
Printed and bound in Great Britain

Park Theatre presents the World Premiere of

Stroke of Luck

by

LARRY BELLING

Cast in Order of Appearance

Monroe Riley	Andrew Langtree
Cory Riley	Kirsty Malpass
Barry Gillis	Jon Glover
Father Riordan	Morgan Deare
Lester Riley	Tim Pigott-Smith
Nurse Lily	Julia Sandiford
Helen Riley	Pamela Miles
Ike Riley	Fergal McElherron
Dr Gunther	Morgan Deare
Ettore Santangelo	Jon Glover

Creative and Production Team

Director	Kate Golledge
Designer	Bob Bailey
Production Manager	Adam Pritchard
Lighting Design	James Whiteside
Sound Design	Theo Holloway
Company Stage Manager	Rachel Reeve
Assistant Stage Mgr	Dan Miller
Costume Supervisor	Daisy Woodroffe
Dialect Coach	Penny Dyer
Press and Publicity	Kate Morley PR

The action of the play takes place a few years ago in and around the town of Huntington, Long Island, New York. There will be one 15-minute interval.

Stroke of Luck was first produced at Park Theatre, Finsbury Park, London on 29 January 2014.

The author wishes to thank the following without whom this production would not have been possible: Davina Belling, Edward Belling, Jeremy Bond, Jez Bond, David Cohen, Melanie and Brad Garnett, Kate Golledge, Mog and Howard Grey, Steve Gunther, Andrew Hainault, Chris and Carolyn Hughes, Stacy Keach, Manny and Willette Klausner, Ellen Krass, Norman Kurland, Jonathan Lynn, Jo and Jeremy Margerison, Richard Melmon, Martha Milliken, Bob and Carol Morris, Marc Norman, Jim Parks, Tim Pigott-Smith, Lonny Price, Beth Uffner, and Ian and Victoria Watson.

Tim Pigott-Smith | Lester Riley

Tim's *King Lear* at the West Yorkshire Playhouse was named by *The Observer* as one of the top ten events of 2011, and his subsequent Prospero in *The Tempest* at the Theatre Royal Bath was likewise acclaimed. One of Britain's busiest actors in all media, Tim's recent TV appearances include *Downton Abbey*, *Woodhouse in Exile*, and *The Great Train Robbery*. His work in radio drama and audio books is extensive including the current *Borgen: Outside the Castle* and H.G. Wells' *The First Men in the Moon*. Tim made his theatre debut with the Bristol Old Vic and went on to many appearances with the RSC and the National. Other roles include *Educating Rita* in the West End working with *Stroke of Luck* director Kate Golledge, *Enron*, *A Delicate Balance*, and *The Iceman Cometh* with Kevin Spacey at the Old Vic and on Broadway. He has also directed major productions of *Hamlet* (Damian Lewis) and *A Royal Hunt of the Sun*. Coming up next is the sci-fi epic movie *Jupiter Ascending* from the directors of *The Matrix*, the role of Asquith in a film about events preceding the First World War called *37 Days*, as an MI6 spy who recruited Houdini in a American TV miniseries, and as George in *Who's Afraid of Virginia Woolf* for the Theatre Royal Bath.

Julia Sandiford | Nurse Lily

Julia trained at Central School of Speech and Drama. She made her stage debut in the UK premiere of *Myth, Propaganda and Disaster in Nazi Germany and Contemporary America* at the Orange Tree Theatre. She has also appeared in Steven Berkoff's production of *Richard II* at the Ludlow and Almagro Festivals, *A Midsummer Night's Dream* at Southwark Playhouse, *Crazy Love* by Che Walker with Paines Plough, *Limehouse Nights* – a devised play about the first London Chinatown – with Kandinsky Theatre, *La Dispute* at Théâtre du Préau in Normandy, *Swallow Song* at Oxford Playhouse and *The Real Thing* at Theatre Royal Bath and on tour. Television includes *Silent Witness, Coronation Street, Hollyoaks* and *Emmerdale*. After taking part in the Unheard Voices writers programme at the Royal Court Theatre she became a founding member of Papergang Theatre, whose aim is to support British East Asian writers. They are currently working on their first production, *BOY* by Tuyen Do. There is more information at www.juliasandiford.co.uk

Andrew Langtree | Monroe Riley

Andrew is originally from St Helens in Lancashire and he graduated among the first alumni of the Liverpool Institute for Performing Arts (LIPA). His West End and professional debut was as Nick Piazza in *Fame* at the Prince of Wales Theatre, before moving slightly north to the Prince Edward Theatre to create the role of Sky in the original cast of *Mamma Mia!* Other West End credits include Eddie in *Blood Brothers* and Carl in the original cast of *Ghost the Musical*. Other theatre credits include roles at the Oldham Coliseum, Theatre Clwyd, the Glasgow Citizens, Birmingham Rep, the West Yorkshire Playhouse, the Bolton Octagon, the Manchester Royal Exchange and the National Theatre (in *The Rose Tattoo*). Screen credits include being a clown with Kevin Kline in the motion picture *De Lovely* and his television roles include *Cutting It, Holby City, Doctors, The Royal, Heartbeat, Coronation Street* and *Emmerdale*.

Kirsty Malpass | Cory

Though born in the UK, Kirsty spent part of her early childhood in New Jersey. After attending the University of Manchester and taking a post-graduate musical theatre degree at Mountview Academy, she made her professional acting debut as Penny the Swan in the Royal National Theatre tour of *Honk!* Other non-human roles followed including a monkey, reindeer, hobbit and, most recently, a Dalmatian with 99 puppies. She welcomes playing a human being again in *Stroke of Luck!* Kirsty's theatre work includes *Chariots of Fire* (Gielgud Theatre), *The Lord of the Rings* (Theatre Royal Drury Lane) *Jerry Springer the Opera* (Cambridge Theatre), *The Sound of Music* (RUG national tour), *It's a Wonderful Life* (UK tour), and in the RSC's *The Wizard of Oz* at both the Birmingham Rep and West Yorkshire Playhouse. A musician as well as an actor (bass, guitar and piano), Kirsty's mezzo soprano voice has been heard on numerous recordings including *The Lord of the Rings* (original London cast recording), and *City Divas* (Masc Records). Her TV appearances include the Mitchell and Webb sitcom *Playing Shop* and she was also seen on the live BBC recording of *Jerry Springer: The Opera*.

Fergal McElherron | Ike Riley

Fergal is both an actor with twenty years' experience and a writer of note. His theatrical play *To Have and To Hold* was nominated for the prestigious Stewart Parker Prize, named after the Belfast playwright, and his two radio plays, *In the Blink of an Eye* and *Prodigal* were produced by RTE, Ireland's public service broadcaster. As an actor he regularly appears at Shakespeare's Globe in such productions as *The Comedy of Errors, As You Like It, Romeo and Juliet, Loves Labour's Lost, A Winter's Tale* and most recently as Quince and the First Fairy in *A Midsummer Night's Dream*. He has also appeared as Nathan Detroit in the Cambridge Arts Theatre production of *Guys and Dolls* and productions at the Tricycle, Abbey Theatre Dublin, the Donmar Warehouse (in *Trelawny of the Wells)*, and the Lyric Theatre Belfast in the two-hander, *Days of Wine and Roses*. He has twice won Best Actor Awards for his work at Dublin Fringe Festivals and was Best Supporting Actor in the Irish Times/ESB Theatre Awards for his work in Voltaire's *Candide*. Fergal is currently writing a new stage play and a TV pilot.

Jon Glover | Barry/Santangelo

Jon originally trained as a teacher at the Central School of Speech and Drama. Following a spell on a kibbutz in Israel he joined schools tours in Yorkshire and Chester gaining his vital Equity Card. London followed with fringe productions, repertory theatre and four years presenting BBC Children's *Play School*. In the West End Jon created Zeppo and understudied Groucho in The Marx Brothers musical *A Day In Hollywood/A Night in the Ukraine*. His first major TV drama role was opposite Tom Wilkinson in *Miss Marple*. His frequent BBC Radio Comedy appearances include many series of *Week Ending*, which led to Central Television's *Spitting Image* and a partnership with Harry Enfield, culminating in Enfield's own TV series in which Jon played Mr Cholmondeley Warner. These days Jon regularly appears in such TV dramas as *Doctors, Midsomer Murders, Foyle's War* and *Casualty*. He is frequently heard on BBC Radio, notably as the villainous Martyn in *The Archers,* and with Bill Nighy in *Charles Paris Mysteries*. Jon will soon be seen in the film version of *London Wall*. He and his wife live near London with four Burmese cats and a Classic 1968 MGC made the same summer he went to drama school.

Morgan Deare | Father Riordan/Dr Gunther

Morgan Deare is one of the most active London-based American actors, working in theatre, TV, film, radio and voiceovers. Born in Louisiana, he moved to London thirty-eight years ago and made his debut in a theatre cabaret of Kurt Weill music. His West End work includes *Little Shop of Horrors*, *A Streetcar Named Desire*, *Whistle Down the Wind* and *South Pacific* amongst others. He was seen off-West End most recently in *Floyd Collins* and *Sweet Smell of Success*. He has appeared in several national tours including *Annie*, *42nd Street*, *Fiddler on the Roof*, *Being Tommy Cooper*, *Carousel* and *Cat on a Hot Tin Roof*, and appeared in numerous provincial theatres in productions such as *Plaza Suite*, *Of Mice and Men*, *Company*, *The Fantasticks* and *Gypsy*. His television appearances include roles in *Nixon's the One*, *Dr Who*, *Coronation Street* and *End Day*. He has played characters in six Radio 4 productions including *Show Boat*, *We Need to Talk About Kevin* and *The Awakening*. His big screen appearances include *Hyde Park on Hudson*, *The Callback Queen* and *Who Framed Roger Rabbit*.

Pamela Miles | Helen Riley

Pamela made her theatre debut in her native Wales in productions for the Welsh Theatre Company including *The Daughter-in-Law*, *The Rivals* and *Antigone*. She has recently been seen in *Utopia* at the Soho Theatre and on tour, *Darker Shores* at the Hampstead Theatre, and with her husband Tim Pigott-Smith in *Pygmalion* for the Peter Hall Company at the Theatre Royal Bath. She has also appeared at the National Theatre in *Animal Farm* and *The Garden of England* and numerous productions at the Old Vic, Royal Court, Gate Theatre, Kings Head and Regent's Park. *King Lear* at the Bristol Old Vic is on her resumé as well as the comedies *Bedroom Farce* and *Habeas Corpus* at the Nottingham Playhouse. She joined the RSC to appear on Broadway in New York in *Sherlock Holmes*. She has been seen on the small screen in *Midsomer Murders*, *Casualty*, *Doctors*, *Rumpole of the Bailey*, *Inspector Morse* and many others, with big screen appearances in *A Fish Called Wanda* and *Under Milk Wood* with Richard Burton and Elizabeth Taylor. Tim and Pamela's son Tom is a noted concert violinist.

Larry Belling | Playwright

Larry worked in radio and theatre in the San Francisco Bay area before starting his career in New York as a theatrical press agent for more than sixty Broadway and off-Broadway shows. In the seventies he publicised films shooting on location in England including *Women in Love* and *The Battle of Britain* and had a side career in the music business managing record producers for groups including The Rolling Stones and Pink Floyd. In Los Angeles in the eighties he wrote and produced Clio Award-winning radio commercials for clients such as American Express, Molson Beers and Greenpeace as well as Hollywood film studios and television networks. He has also narrated documentaries for PBS, Discovery Channel and the BBC, and voiced numerous commercials. Larry's online tools for writers, including the web's only slang thesaurus, can be found at www.writersdreamtools.com and he created a successful iPad/iPhone app called HistoryTools, a daily calendar of historical events going back 2,000 years. *Stroke of Luck* is Larry's first play and is based on a true incident in his life. He lives in London and on a lake in the Catskills with his wife, the film and TV producer Davina Belling.

Kate Golledge | Director

Kate trained as a director at the Liverpool Institute for the Performing Arts, and early in her career she was a finalist in the JMK Trust Award, presented annually to a promising young director, for her conceptual production of Arthur Miller's *The Crucible*. Her recent directing credits include *Red Riding Hood* and Roald Dahl's *Fantastic Mr Fox* for the Singapore Repertory Theatre, for whom she will be directing *The Emperor and the Nightingale* later this year. Other credits include *The Road to Qatar!* at the Landor and Edinburgh Festivals, *Parade* and *Spring Awakening* at the Pleasance, London, and *Men Are from Mars, Women Are from Venus* in Edinburgh and on tour in the UK. Kate has also directed a new musical adaptation of *Passport to Pimlico* performed on the streets of Pimlico as part of SouthWestFest, and a promenade production of *Carmen* for Opera La Goziniere. Kate was Resident/Associate Director at the London Palladium (*The Wizard of Oz*) and the Menier Chocolate Factory and West End productions of *Sweet Charity, Shirley Valentine* and *Educating Rita,* which starred Tim Pigott-Smith. Visit her website at *www.kategolledge.co.uk*

Bob Bailey | Designer

Bob Bailey has designed sets and costumes for theatres all over Europe and England including the Royal Court, Liverpool Everyman, Hampstead Theatre, Crucible Sheffield, The Bush and Theatre Royal Old Vic. He recently returned from Vienna where he designed *The Woman in Black* and from Copenhagen where he did the sets for *La Cage Aux Folles* for the Aarhus Theatre. He has also designed *All Nighter* and *Horseplay* for the Royal Ballet and for many operas in Holland Park, London, Guildhall Opera, British Youth Opera and Nationale Reisopera in the Netherlands. His designs for *Anything Goes, Lieutenant of Inishmore* and Tom Stoppard's *The Real Thing* have been seen on national tours and he did the set for the Take That musical *Never Forget* at the Savoy Theatre in London and on two tours. Bob was awarded Time Out Designer of the Year in 1999 for his set design for the UK and European tours of DV8's *The Happiest Day of My Life*.

James Whiteside | Lighting Designer

James has over ten years' experience as a lighting designer. As well as work in the West End, he has lit productions for the Chichester Festival Theatre, Library Theatre in Manchester, Mercury Theatre in Colchester, Citizen's Theatre Glasgow, Perth Theatre, Lyric Theatre, Belfast, Salisbury Playhouse, West Yorkshire Playhouse, Rose Theatre, Bush Theatre, St James Theatre and the Print Room. James has worked extensively on productions for a younger audience with the Tall Stories Theatre Company, Chichester Festival Youth Theatre, Chicken Shed, Birmingham Stage Company and Theatre Royal Bath.

Adam Pritchard | Production Manager

Adam graduated Middlesex University with a BA (Hons) in Drama and Theatre Arts and the Central School of Speech and Drama with an MA in Music Theatre. Adam is Technical Manager of Park Theatre where he has worked on *These Shining Lives, Daytona, Adult Supervision* and *Sleeping Beauty*. Previously he was Deputy Chief Electrician of the Dominion Theatre in London's West End, home to *We Will Rock You*. He has also worked at Trafalgar Studios, Aldwych Theatre, Lyceum Theatre, Royal Albert Hall and Lyric Hammersmith. Lighting design credits include *Volpone* (Upstairs/Gatehouse), *Peter*

Pan (UK tour), *The Audition* (Barons Court), *Punk Rock, Top Girls* and *Great Expectations* (Tristan Bates), *Deep Cut/Stories For Boys* (Landor), *Summit Conference* (New Wimbledon Studio), *My Best Friend* (Courtyard), *Vagina Monologues* (Upstairs/Gatehouse). Adam is also Artistic Director of Hidden Talent Productions and co-wrote/produced *Heaven Sent* at the New Wimbledon Studio.

Theo Holloway | Sound Design

Theo has more than sixty professional credits as a sound designer and composer including many of the Park Theatre's first season productions and four seasons at the Scoop at More London. Among his projects were *Hedda Gabler, Spring Awakening, Romeo and Juliet, Macbeth* and *Hamlet* (UK tour for Icarus Theatre), *Charley Bear's Christmas Adventure* (The Ambassador's Theatre), *Men Are from Mars, Women Are from Venus* (UK tour, Edinburgh), *Gutted, Shalom Baby, The Graft, Two Women, There's Something About Simmi* (Theatre Royal Stratford East), *Third Floor* (Trafalgar Studios), *The Moon is Halfway to Heaven* (Jermyn Street Theatre), *Parade* (Southwark Playhouse), *Sign of the Times* (Duchess Theatre – Musical Arrangements), *Corrie!* (The Lowry), *A Plague Over England* (Duchess Theatre) and pantomimes for Qdos, First Family, Newbury Corn Exchange and Theatre Royal Stratford East. He also works as a technical consultant and developer for live sound, specialising in radio frequency engineering.

① Stroke of Luck Company: Morgan
Deare, Kirsty Malpass, Julia
Sandiford, Fergal McElherron,
Jon Glover, Pamela Miles, Andrew
Langtree and Tim Pigott-Smith
② Tim Pigott-Smith as Lester Riley
③ Kirsty Malpass
④ Tim Pigott-Smith and Julia
Sandiford
⑤ Rehearsing scene one
⑥ Director Kate Golledge and
playwright Larry Belling
⑦ Pamela Miles and Tim Pigott-Smith
⑧ Andrew Langtree and Fergal
McElherron as Monroe and Ike

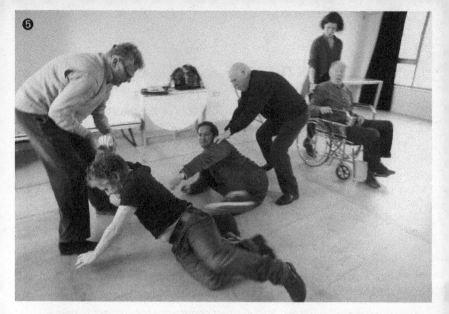

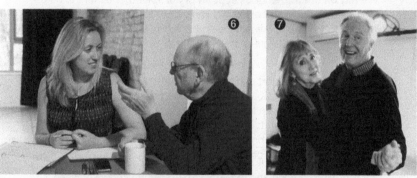

Photographs by Howard Grey

ABOUT PARK THEATRE

'A spanking new five-star neighbourhood theatre' Independent

Opened in May 2013, Park Theatre consists of two theatres – with 200 seats and 90 seats respectively – plus a dedicated community learning space, an all day cafe-bar and ancillary facilities.

With a broad artistic policy encompassing both classics and new writing and an ambitious outreach programme, Park Theatre sits at the heart of its community.

'A first-rate new theatre in north London' Daily Telegraph

Park Theatre is a registered charity (number 1137223) and receives no public subsidy. Ticket sales alone are not enough to cover the running costs and it is only through your support that we can keep the theatre thriving.

We rely on the tremendous support of our volunteer ushers to help staff the building – and enjoy including them in the Park family. If you're local and would like to volunteer as an usher then we'd love to hear from you. Please email our Front of House Manager on foh@parktheatre.co.uk

If you're able to support us financially there are many ways from donating just £1 with your ticket booking to becoming a friend, naming a seat and even legacy giving – many of these come with an exciting array of benefits including priority booking, private tours and receptions. To discuss how you can support us please email our Development Director on development@parktheatre.co.uk

For more information and the latest on upcoming shows please visit the website: parktheatre.co.uk

We look forward to seeing you again soon.
Very best wishes,

Jez Bond
Artistic Director

SUPPORTERS

Great Friends

Robert Albury
Dr Linda Almond
Anderson Bakewell
Simon Birt
Gemma Birt
Jane Birt
Greetje Brosens
Chris Bulford
Tim Burley
Frances Carlisle
James Carroll
Emily Clark
Helen Clements
Teresa Curnew
Colin Davey
Malcolm Downing
Wendy Edgar-Jones
Eion Doran
Robert Gill
Sheila Gillard
Dawn Green
Richard Harris
Patrick Hort
Samantha James
Antoine Josset
Aleksander Kuczynski
Patrizia Lillus
Victoria Little
Helen Llewelyn
Linda Logan
Rachel Lush
Rebecca Mackinney
George McGeorge
Andrew Merriam
Dr Jonathan Myers
Alexander Nash
Jamie Pantling
Andrew Pattison
Richard Philips
Kate Poynton
Nicola Price

Diane Reay
Phil Reedy
Heinz Richardson
Clare Richmond
Claire Robinson
Frieda Schicker
Lisa Seidel
Ben Shaw
Karen Sims
Socrates Socratous
Chloe Squires
Peter Svoboda
Maria Tuck
Liz Whitlock

Wonderful Friends

Christian Abletshauser
Tony Alveranga
Gillian Auld
Leo Avery
Ray Barker
Helen Baron
Alexander Beetles
John Bertram
Jacques Bingham
Dr Maria Bitner-Glindzicz
Mark Bradley
Susan Bradley
Edward Bretherton
June Burrows
Anne-Marie Cameron
Caroline Conlon
Richard Dayman
Ian Dench
Aimie Drinkwater
Katherine Elizabeth McLean
Angela Ferns
Simon Fuchs
William Gaminara
Virginia Garcia

Sean Garvey
Anne-Marie Hargreaves
Scott Harrison
David Harrison
William Hibbert
Rowan Howard
The Jones Family
Sara Keene
Matthew Kelly
Hilary King
Nathaniel Lalone
Linda Long
Keith Mason
Kieran McCloskey
Liviu Morariu
Sara Oliver
Mark Owen
Helen Rowe
Kevin Shen
Andrew Shepherd
Francesca Simon
Adrian Smith
Justina Stewart
Patrick Stewart
Will Stowell
Paula Swift
Robert Timms
Harvey Trollope
Julia Tsybina
Sharon Vanloo
Maria Vasina
Richard Whitaker
Suzanne Wilcox
Gaynor Wilson
Jane Yeager
Nora Zaragoza Valero

Best Friends

Scott and Claire Mackin

Stroke of Luck

Characters

Lester Riley – *a retired television repairman, resident of Bayside Manor Retirement Home.*
Monroe (Munny) – *his oldest son. A Certified Public Accountant.*
Ike – *his second son. Released from jail a year ago, he makes ends meet.*
Corinne (Cory) – *his daughter, an obsessive compulsive with a germ phobia.*
Nurse Lily Hashimoto – *a young, smart, sexy nurse, from Japan.*
Helen Riley – *Lester's wife, deceased.*

The same actor plays these roles:

Barry Gillis – *next-door neighbor of the Riley family.*
Ettore Santangelo – *a self-made man and former customer of Lester's.*

The same actor plays these roles:

Father Riordan – *a Catholic Priest.*
Dr Gunther – *the administrator of Bayside Manor.*
(Or vice versa.)

Act 1

Scene 1 – The living room of Barry Gillis in Huntington, Long Island, NY.
Scene 2 – The garden at Bayside Manor Retirement Home – the next morning.
Scene 3 – Monroe's office – a few days later.
Scene 4 – Lester's room at Bayside Manor – the next day.
Scene 5 – The office of Dr Gunther, chief adminstrator.
Scene 6 – Lester's room at Bayside Manor.

Act 2

Scene 1 – Lester's room at Bayside Manor – two weeks later.
Scene 2 – The Rectory at St Hugh's Catholic Church – a few days later.
Scene 3 – Monroe's home in Huntington, LI.
Scene 4 – The Santangelo Mansion in Huntington, LI – a few days later.
Scene 5 – Lester's room at Bayside Manor – a few days later.
Scene 6 – The living room of Barry Gillis – a month later.

Scenic note: The scenery should be fluid with no long scene changes and mostly indicated with furnishings and lighting. Painted Japanese screens or projections may be used.

Act One

Scene One

Barry Gillis's *middle-class living room in a Long Island suburb. A brass urn sits on the mantelpiece. Upstage left is a bathroom with a sink and toilet. It would be nice if they were functional but sound effects and a lighting effect would suffice. There is a SFX of a small crowd mingling from the audience.* **Monroe** *and* **Cory** *wander onstage separately.* **Monroe**, *wearing a boring grey suit and tie, consults his watch.* **Cory** *looks out at the audience.*

Cory (*to* **Monroe**)   It's a good turn-out for Mother.

Monroe   Even the Shains are here.

Cory   She looks good.

Monroe   Her plastic surgeon is a master.

Cory   Uncle Paddy seems upset.

Monroe   He's a sourpuss.

Cory (*under her breath*)   Asshole.

Monroe   He's not even our real uncle.

Cory   You're unbelievable.

Monroe   There's Manny Klausner. I wish I could get his account. He's rolling in it.

Cory   You're not going to hustle for business *here*!

Monroe (*fed up with her*)   I'm certainly going to talk to him. Why the hell shouldn't I?

Cory   Because it is not the time or the place . . .

Barry Gillis *enters, carrying a precariously loaded tray of clinking glasses. He is totally bald and wears overalls.* **Cory** *and* **Monroe** *watch him fumble with the glasses.*

Monroe   What do you wanna bet he drops them?

Cory   Nothing, but I bet *you* ten bucks he says a cliché within one minute.

Monroe   Naw . . .

Cory   Okay, a cliché plus something in his lousy Spanish.

Monroe   One minute. You're on.

Monroe *checks his watch and goes over to* **Barry** *trying to balance the glasses.*

Monroe   Hi, Barry. Let me take those for you.

Barry (*handing him the tray of glasses*)   Muchas gracias, Munny. Oh hi, Cory, how's tricks?

Cory (*to* **Monroe**)   Six seconds. Pay up. Ten bucks.

Monroe   I uh . . . don't think I have any cash on me.

Barry   You need some dinero, Munny? I can loan you ten bucks.

Cory   No, he doesn't need a loan, Barry. How are you keeping anyway?

Barry   Muy bueno. I just hope I have enough stuff to eat and drink.

Monroe *takes the tray of glasses and puts it on a table.*

Cory   I'm just going to the bathroom.

Monroe   Father will be here any minute. Don't stay in there all day, Sis.

Cory   Why do you still talk to me like I'm a child? I haven't even seen you for three years!

Monroe   You saw me at the funeral for the two minutes you weren't in the bathroom.

Cory   You just don't know when to stop, do you?

Cory *rushes to the bathroom and begins washing her hands furiously in the sink.*

Monroe (*to* **Barry**)   It's really nice of you to have Mother's memorial here.

Barry   Don't mention it, Munny. You lived next door for almost twenty years.

Monroe   I wish you'd call me Monroe, Barry. I'm not a kid anymore.

Barry   I remember when you were little. You and your brother played with my Tommy in your basement.

Monroe   We called it the 'ruckus room'.

Barry   You got into fights down there, mano-a-mano. Ike didn't pull any punches.

Monroe   Nobody got hurt. Swearing, bad names, smoking. Just kid's stuff.

Barry   What was that funny peculiar name Ike used to call you? Fossi? Fossel?

Monroe   It was, uh, Fossa, or something like that.

Barry   Porque?

Monroe   I dunno.

Barry   Is Ike coming today?

Monroe   We haven't seen or heard from him since he got out. Excuse me. I'm just going to see if Father's van is in sight. They're driving him over from the Manor.

Father Riordan *enters almost bumping into* **Monroe** *exiting.*

Father Riordan   Oh hello, Monroe. Haven't seen you in church . . .

Monroe (*rushing out the door*)   Not now, Father.

Barry *comes over.*

Barry   Howdy, Padre, qué pasa?

Father Riordan   Nothing new, Mr Gillis, just life and death, la vida y la muerte.

Barry   Que?

Father Riordan   Lester's not here yet?

Barry   Munny just went to see if his car is comin' round the bend.

Father Riordan   I took a taxi from St Hugh's. Haven't been around here since he had his stroke.

Barry   The day after his retirement party. Hard to believe.

Father Riordan   Especially for someone so young.

Barry   Rotten luck, and now Helen. Who would've thought she would go first?

Father Riordan (*crossing himself*)   Not me. (*Changing the subject.*) The old neighborhood looks pretty good.

Barry   We keep it clean, but the mansions up the street are starting to look a bit run-down.

Father Riordan   Do those same Italian families live there – Indelicato . . . Santangelo?

Barry   Yeah, but they keep to themselves.

Father Riordan   They seem to have found another parish.

Barry   Can't win 'em all. Are you going to put in your two cents worth today?

Father Riordan   Yes, Helen was indeed a charitable woman.

Barry   I should try to visit Lester more often. It's been some time.

Father Riordan   I see him every week for communion.

Barry   The last time I saw him he could hardly move. His left side was almost paralyzed.

Father Riordan   He has made great improvements in a year.

Barry   He couldn't hear me very well.

Father Riordan   He's got a hearing aid for his left ear and the rehab sessions have helped. And thank the good Lord his mouth doesn't slant to the left side any more.

Cory *finally finishes washing her hands and turns off the tap. She looks at the towels in the bath disdainfully, and pulls toilet paper off the roll to dry her hands. She enters the room.*

Cory   Hello, Father.

Father Riordan   You're looking very nice, Corinne.

Cory   Thank you. (*Indicating audience.*) Mother would have been surprised to see all these people.

Father Riordan   She had a lot of friends.

Cory (*sarcastically*)   Yes, she was good to her *friends*.

Barry   She was just what the doctor ordered.

Cory   She was always running off to help some unfortunate child.

Barry   She was a classy dame, a real peach.

Father Riordan   Good mother.

Cory   Sure. Wonderful.

Father Riordan   I understand you have a concern about cleanliness, Corinne. My sister's eldest is a doctor . . .

Cory   Don't worry about me, Father. I'm just fine. Okay?

Father Riordan   I know it's hard to lose a mother . . .

Cory   Well, actually it's not really . . . excuse me, Father.

Cory *ducks away from the* **Priest**. **Monroe** *enters hurriedly.*

Monroe   His van's just pulling up to the curb. Obviously he'll be feeling depressed, so I think we should give him a round of applause when he comes in.

Cory   Isn't that somewhat inappropriate?

Monroe   What the hell's the matter with a show of respect?

Cory   This is a memorial service for Mother, not Papa.

Lester *is in a wheelchair and is pushed by a uniformed nurse who keeps her head down and avoids looking at anyone. She pushes him to the center of the stage, turns him towards the audience and locks his chair in place. She goes over to a dark side of the stage and sits.* **Lester** *wears a grey jogging outfit, a baseball cap and white running shoes. There is a colorful blanket on his lap.*

Lester (*to audience*)   Thank you all for coming.

Father Riordan   It's me, Lester. How are you coping?

Lester   I'm fine, Father. Top of the world. (*To audience.*) Everyone knows Father Riordan?

Monroe *goes over and shakes hands with the* **Priest**.

Monroe   You're very kind to come, Father.

Father Riordan   I've prepared a few words.

Monroe   That would be really nice.

Lester   Barry, thank you for opening your home to us.

Barry   Mi casa es su casa, Lester.

Lester (*pointing with his good right hand to his left ear*)   Say what? Could you turn up my hearing aid?

Barry *twiddles* **Lester**'s *volume control.*

Barry (*very loudly into* **Lester**'s *ear*)   How's that?

Lester (*somewhat painfully*)   Much better, Barry. Do you still have that Admiral radio I gave you out of my repair shop?

Barry   Of course. It's a real doozy.

Lester   Could I have a drink?

Barry   Name your poison.

Lester   How about a double gin? And put a drop of sake in it.

Barry   Sakee?

Lester   Japanese rice wine.

Barry   I don't think I have any, but I'll take a look.

Barry *exits.*

Lester   Monroe. You did a good job getting everyone here.

Cory   Hi, Papa.

Lester   Cory. You came. I'm glad.

Cory   Of course I'm here, Papa.

Lester   How about Franklin?

Cory   No, Papa. He doesn't know.

Lester   You haven't told your own brother yet?

Cory   You know what he's like, Papa. He doesn't understand things the same way we do.

Lester   One of the volunteers at the home should have brought him here.

Cory   I know it's a sad day, Papa.

Lester (*a choked laugh*)   I want to be happy.

Cory   Since your stroke, I can't tell if you're laughing or crying.

Lester   If I have tears in my eyes it is probably laughter.

Barry *returns and hands* **Lester** *his drink.*

Lester   Arigato, Barry.

Barry   What?

Lester   Arigato. That's Japanese for thank you.

Barry   I didn't have any sakee. I gave you straight gin.

Lester   Kanpai.

Barry   Salud.

Lester *holds the drink in his good right hand and sips slowly through a straw.* **Monroe** *comes downstage to the apron dragging a chair. He sits and addresses the audience.*

Monroe   Uh. Let's get started shall we?

Small crowd SFX out.

We're here to pay our respects to our mother, Helen Riley, and remember her memory and her good works, especially with children. Most of our family is around us. My two boys, Bob and Roger, are stuck at school, but they send you love, Father.

Lester   They should'a made the effort. Hey, have you heard my good news?

Cory (*taken aback*)   Shhh. Papa.

Monroe   I know that many of you have memories you want to share today. But first I'd like to say a few things about Mother that perhaps some of you didn't know. She and Father were childhood sweethearts and got married when they were only twenty-three. When Father had his stroke Mother found him on the floor of the bathroom and used her nurse's training to take care of him. When it became too much for her she sold the house and they moved to Bayside Manor.

Except for a light on **Lester** *and the urn, the lights dim quickly.* **Monroe** *freezes.* **Helen** *appears and puts her arms around* **Lester** *from behind. He suddenly seems like a much younger man.*

Lester   Helen? Is that you?

Helen   I'm here.

Lester *rises gingerly and embraces her.*

Lester   What the hell is he going on about, Helen?

Helen   Talking nonsense – I never trained as a nurse.

Lester   You were a good one though. You did everything for me.

Helen   Everything I could.

Lester   Munny never really knew you.

Helen   Or you.

Lester   I was a good father to him.

Helen   You did your best.

Lester   Whenever Munny comes over now he pressures me to make him executor.

Helen   But you don't trust him.

Lester   I used to say to him, 'Munny doesn't make the world go 'round.'

Helen   Very clever, dear.

Lester   He didn't get it.

Helen   He seldom did.

Lester   He broke my favorite record and never apologized.

Helen   I'm sure he didn't mean to.

Lester   The nurses tell me he tries to hit on them.

Helen   Foolish man, but at least he gave us grandchildren.

Lester   They're just like *him*. They came around after your cremation – ignored me and played touch football on the grass.

Helen   Have you heard from Ike?

Lester   No sign of him.

Helen   What about Franklin?

Lester   He doesn't know yet.

Helen   You can't let him rot in that place, Lester.

Lester   I can't exactly jump in the Plymouth and take him bowling.

Helen   He must be told. He's had a hard time.

Lester   We did our best. We took him to church almost every Sunday.

Helen   Franklin loved St Hugh's. He used to draw pictures of Father Riordan with a long beard.

Lester   He played my Jimmy Durante record over and over again until Munny broke it.

Helen (*sings*)   'Make Someone Happy.'

Lester   I want to be happy too, Helen.

Helen   You deserve it, Lester. You're still young.

Lester   I may not be in great shape but I'm going to make my move.

Helen   What's in that devious mind of yours?

Lester   Something devious.

Helen   Do you know what you're doing?

Lester   Yes. I've been thinking about it ever since you left.

Helen   Are you going to tell me what it is?

Lester   You'll see.

Helen   When?

Lester   Soon.

Helen   You've always been bull-headed.

Lester   I hope it won't upset you.

Helen   It's far too late for that.

Lester   Stay with me. I need your help.

Helen   Why?

Lester   I've never done anything without you. Please don't go. I miss you.

Helen *disappears and* **Lester** *slips into his wheelchair, an invalid again. The lights come up and the light on the urn fades.* **Monroe** *is finishing his praise of his mother.*

Monroe   . . . so that gives you a little idea of how respected Mother was in the area of child care for retards, er . . . retarded persons and autistic, dyslexic, whatever. And now I'll turn the floor over to my sister Corinne. Cory . . .

Cory (*monotone rambling*)   When I was a little girl I worshipped my mother. I thought she was a saint, holier than a nun.

Ike *comes reeling into the room. He is drunk. He stares at his sister and gives a little wave acknowledging the audience.*

Cory   She expected a lot of me . . . and I tried my best to be as perfect as she was, but I had my uh, health issues, and she was busy with her charities and we were never really part of that after Franklin went to the home, and . . .

Ike *goes into the bathroom and throws up noisily in the toilet.*

Cory   . . . I think she was happy I became a teacher but we never really connected after . . . well now that she's gone I'll be here for you more, Papa, Yeah, that's what I need to do. I loved my mother a lot. She was a great person, I guess.

Monroe (*to audience*)   Thank you, Cory. We are most grateful to Father Riordan who will give a eulogy and a blessing. Father.

Father Riordan *goes to center stage and takes out a paper to read, adjusts his glasses and opens his mouth to speak . . .*

Cory (*aside to* **Monroe**)   Why don't you go help your brother?

Monroe   Why don't you?

Father Riordan (*to audience*)   When a dear friend dies it is time for . . .

Cory (*hissing at* **Monroe**)   He's drunk. Can't you get him out of here?

Father Riordan   . . . reflection on all our lives. When someone as charitable as Helen dies . . .

Ike *flushes the toilet and comes staggering out of the bathroom.*
Father Riordan *pauses, confused, waiting for quiet.*

Ike   Well, that's better. Touch of the old indigestion.

Father Riordan *wonders whether he should continue or sit down.*
Ike *leans on him for support and the* **Priest** *almost collapses.*

Ike   Hey, Father. How's it hanging? (*To* **Monroe**.) Hiya, Fossa. (*To* **Cory**.) How are the germs today, Cory? How's it going? Everybody sad? I'd like to say a few words about dear departed mummy. Let's see. What can I say? Where was she most of the time? Playing games with a bunch of spastics.

Cory   Stop it, Ike.

Ike   Isn't this a wake? Why is Pop drinking and nobody else? I'll have a tequila on the rocks.

Monroe   This is not a wake, you little shit, it's a memorial service for our mother.

Cory   Please, Ike. (*To audience.*) Please excuse him.

Monroe (*to* **Ike**)   Sit down and put a lid on it.

Ike   Oh, sorry, sorry. I'll try to think of something nice. Mummy, mummy. Yeah, maybe we should wrap her in towels like an Egyptian mummy. (*Spotting urn.*) Oh I see it's too late for that.

Monroe   Lay off it, Ike.

Ike   You're right. This isn't a time for jokes. How's it goin', Pop?

Lester   Ikey. I never expected you.

Ike   Yeah, it's me, Pop.

Lester   I'm pleased to see you.

Ike   Why is that, Pop?

Lester   I want you to hear my good news.

Ike   Mother's dead. That's *bad* news, isn't it? Why would you . . .

Lester   Shut up for a minute and I'll tell you. I want everybody to know. (*Indicating audience with his good right arm.*)

Ike   Okay, I'm all shut up, Pop. (*Mimes zippering his mouth.*) So what is your good news?

Pause.

Lester   The good news is . . . I . . . I . . . I'm getting mmm . . .

Ike   Spit it out, Pop.

Father Riordan (*cheerfully*)   What he's trying to say is that he's getting married again!

Barry   Que?!

Cory   Say what?

Monroe   Now I've heard everything.

Ike (*breaks up laughing*)   That's funny, Pop. Who's the lucky vestal virgin?

Lester   I'm marrying Lily. Everybody is invited to the wedding.

Cory (*to the* **Priest**)   Father, can't you make him . . .

Lester   It's alright, Cory. Father Riordan is going to perform the service.

Father Riordan   . . . and it will be a great honor.

Ike   Who is this Lily, Pop? Some old crone at Bedside Manor?

Lester   *Bayside* Manor. You don't know her.

Ike (*slurring his words*)   I want to meet her. Shildren should be able to give their approval. Where is she?

Lester   Come over here, Lily.

Lester *gestures to his nurse with his good arm. She rises and walks over to* **Lester**'s *wheelchair.*

Here she is, your future step-mother.

She takes off her nurses hat and a cascade of black hair tumbles down her shoulders. She is gorgeous. She is Japanese. **Cory** *rushes into the bathroom, turns on the tap and washes her hands through the end of the scene.*

Ike   Jesus, Pop. Who's going to consummate the marriage? Munny? I bet he's fucked most of the other nurses.

Monroe   You liar!

Monroe *grabs* **Ike** *by the shoulders and forces him to the ground. He beats his brother's head on the ground.* **Barry** *and* **Father Riordan** *try unsuccessfully to pull him off.*

Monroe   How dare you say that in front of our friends and neighbors? You son of a bitch.

Ike   I don't believe you're really my brother. You must be the son of another bitch!

Monroe   You finally turn up after all this time and what do you do? Insult all of us and the memory of your mother . . .

Lester   Stop. Stop fighting. I don't need Munny to consummate the marriage.

Monroe *stops banging* **Ike**'s *head on the ground and looks up at his father.*

Monroe   What did he say?

Father Riordan   He is perfectly able to consummate the marriage himself.

Monroe   He is?

Ike   How, Pop?

Lester   I told you – only the left side of my penis is paralyzed!

Beat. Blackout.

Scene Two

Music cue: A Koto arpeggio. A sign says: 'Bayside Manor – Keep off the grass.' **Lily** *pushes* **Lester**'s *wheelchair across downstage.*

Lester   Wheel me into the sunlight, Lily. Let me feel the sun on my face.

Lily   How about here, Rester?

We will omit the Japanese accent spelling from now on.

Lester   Here is good.

She stops him in a pool of light. She removes his baseball cap so his face gets the sun.

Lily   Ogenki desu ka?

Lester   How am I? Genki desu, arigato gozaimaysu.

Lily   Good. But it is pronounced goza*imah*su.

Lester   Arigato goza*imah*su. Thank you very much.

Lily   Or more simply, domo, informal, like thanks.

Lester   Domo. You're a good sport, Lily. You're my little geisha girl.

Lily   You're my big samurai.

Lester   I should be so lucky.

Lily   You are lucky. You have me to look after you.

Lester   When I heard that a Japanese nurse was coming to work here I told Dr Gunther I needed you.

Lily   Why was that?

Lester   When I was in the Navy in '62 I was stationed for a while in the Port of Tokyo waiting for Vietnam to happen. One Sunday I met a nice girl named Michiko at church. I tried to learn a few words of Japanese so I could talk to her but I just couldn't grasp it. A few months with you and it's coming nicely.

Lily   You're trying harder.

Lester   I loved your homeland, the people, the culture. It was so . . . harmonious.

Lily   Less crime.

Lester   Japan has two hundred less murders every year than America.

Lily   And there are thirty times more prisoners in jail here than in Japan.

Lester   Why do you think?

Lily   Strong families. Strong fathers.

Lester (*smiles*)   We gave my family a good shock yesterday, didn't we?

Lily   Our wedding will give them a bigger shock.

Lester *laughs.*

Lily   There's an old Japanese proverb that says 'Never leave your offspring unattended within twisted branches'.

Lester   That's what I want to do – untwist my children's branches.

Lily   I will help you. Tell me what to do.

Lester   Nothing right away. Our announcement must simmer for a little while.

Lily   Are you hungry?

Lester   I can always eat.

Lily   I will make you special sashimi like my father taught me.

Lester   Your father was a good cook?

Lily   He is a chef, a professional.

Lester   What was he like as a father?

Lily   He was fair but strict. He always treated us as adults, even when we were little children. We were poor, but we always thought we were rich.

Lester   He sounds just like me. I was a good father too. A good father gives children independence and teaches them self-reliance.

Lily   Japanese fathers can take a test and write an essay to prove their parenting skills. My father was tops in his class.

Lester   I would have scored well too.

Lily   He is still humble today even though he is one of the few chefs in Kobe to receive a government license to serve fugu, or as some pronounce it, 'fuku'.

Lester   Fookoo?

Lily   It's a puffer fish or blow fish. Some of its organs contain tetrodotoxin.

Lester   What is that?

Lily   A poison that causes paraplegia and even asphyxiation leading to death.

Lester   Why would anybody eat that?

Lily   The blow fish gives a wonderful tingling sensation on the tongue and lips. Some say it is better than sex.

Lester   In my condition anything like sex is good. Blow . . . fish . . .

Lester *ponders other types of 'blow . . . '*

Lily (*laughs*)   It's not quite the same, I'm sure. You must taste fuku. I will ask my father to FedEx some here.

She wipes his brow with a cold compress.

Lester (*counting syllables on his fingers*)   I await fuku
   As children untwist branches
   And shit hits the fan

Lily   At last you have made a splendid haiku.

Lester   Haiku, fugu, fuku, everything nice in Japanese seems to end in ooo.

Lily   Ai shiteru.

Lester   That too ends in ooo.

Lily   It means 'I love you'.

Lester   Do you love me, Lily?

She smiles warmly as the lights fade on **Lester**'s *beaming face.*

Scene Three

Monroe's *office downtown.* **Monroe** *in his usual grey suit and boring tie is apoplectic on the speaker phone.*

Monroe   What do you mean client privilege, Peccorino? I'm his oldest son. Send me his books. (*Pause.*) I'm warning you, Gil. Your father was a good man, but you are being unfair. (*Pause.*) No, you've got it wrong there, pal. I don't care if my father signed a hundred-year agreement with your firm, I'm going to have it declared null and void. See you in court, you bastard.

He slams down the phone. It immediately rings and he answers.

Monroe   What? (*Pause.*) Tell him to go away, I'm busy.

Monroe *shuffles papers around his desk. After a beat,* **Ike** *bursts through the door.*

Ike   What do you mean you're busy? Too busy to see your fuckin' brother?

Monroe   Civilized people call for an appointment. They knock on the door first.

Ike   You're a jerk, Fossa.

Monroe   Alright, sit down. What do you want?

Ike   I thought we oughta catch up.

Ike *sits.* **Monroe** *shuffles more papers, putting one stack on the other and then shifting them a filing cabinet behind him.* **Ike** *puts his feet on the desk.*

Monroe   So what have you been doing since you got out?

Ike   A little of this, a little of that. Working out at the gym. Making ends meet. That's what I want to talk to you about. I've got some ideas . . .

Monroe   Don't ask me for any money, Ike. I've got two boys in private school.

Ike   I need thirty grand.

Monroe   In your dreams.

Ike   Twenty?

Monroe   I'm paying alimony. Give me a break.

Ike   Like you ever gave me a break?

Monroe *finishes shuffling at the filing cabinet and notices* **Ike**'s *feet on the desk.*

Monroe   And get your feet off my desk. Where do you think you are, back in Rikers?

Ike   I was at the Elmira Correctional Facility near Binghamton up Route 17, Fossa. Only three hours tops and you never visited me once.

Monroe   I was busy.

Ike   Bullshit. Cory came three times. Mother twice. She tried to bring Franklin once but he started throwing up when they hit the Catskills.

Monroe   Franklin. He used to scare me with his tantrums and spinning around in circles.

Ike   Remember how he would grab a pencil and paper and write his name over and over again? I was relieved when they put him in that home.

Monroe   You were mean to him.

Ike   Bullshit. I once told him he couldn't cut the mustard. He dumped a jar of mustard on the table and started hacking it with a knife.

Monroe   You pushed him around. You hit him.

Ike (*ignoring the accusation*)   I used to wish he was a savant like the fuckin' Rain Man. I could have taken him to Atlantic City and won a bundle at blackjack. But he sure wasn't. Do you ever see him?

Monroe   Mother made me come to his birthday a few years ago. You?

Ike   I haven't exactly been available, have I?

Monroe (*badgering him*)   You've been out for a year. What've you been doing? You're not up to your old tricks again, are you? Because if you are you can just get the hell right outa here.

Ike   I'll give you a tip, Fossa. If you have a really bad cough? Take a large dose of laxatives. Then you'll be afraid to cough.

Monroe   What the hell is that supposed to mean?

Ike   Oh forget it. (*Pause.*) Hey, you want to hear something funny? Guess who was in the next cell to mine?

Monroe   I give up.

Ike   Gianni Santangelo.

Monroe   The kid down the street who beat you up?

Ike   He didn't beat me up.

Monroe   He put you in the hospital with a concussion.

Ike   I was in for two hours for observation, it wasn't a concussion.

Monroe   Yeah, sure.

Ike   We hit it off big time me and Gianni. He turned into a really, really nice stand-up guy. Salt of the earth. A good soul.

Monroe   What's he in for?

Ike   Rape.

Monroe   Rape?

Ike   It was a set-up job. Theresa Scalise lied on the stand.

Monroe   That bimbo!

Ike   You had her in the ruckus room, didn't you?

Monroe   No, it was her sister. And listen, you asshole, how dare you tell our friends and neighbors about my having sex with anyone?

Ike   I was drunk. It was a joke.

Monroe   Not funny, McGee. You insulted me.

Ike   Oh c'mon, Fossa. You know you fuck around. You cheat on everyone.

Monroe   I do not. You're the criminal. I'm the honest one.

Ike   Ha! You honest? What about grandpa's coin collection?

Monroe   What about it?

Ike   When he died, you took all the silver dollars. There must have been a hundred of them.

Monroe   Naw, there were only about forty. They were stolen when our first house was burgled.

Ike   The point is you took the dollars and gave me the pennies. You were cheating me.

Monroe   Those were Indian Head Pennies, Ike. One was a 1909S that was worth more than all the silver dollars put together.

Ike (*caustically*)   It was worn down so far you could hardly see fuckin' Tonto. So listen, what are we going to do about Casanova?

Monroe   Who?

Ike   Don Juan.

Monroe   Who?

Ike   Pop!

Monroe   Oh. I've got to figure out a way to get the books.

Ike   You don't have the books?

Monroe   No.

Ike   Why not? You're a CPA.

Monroe   When his accountant Peccorino died I pleaded with Father to let me take over.

Ike   And . . .

Monroe   The next day he turned over everything to Peccorino's son, Gil. I was at school with him. He could barely use a calculator.

Ike   Didn't trust you, did he? How much are we talking about anyway?

Monroe   Okay, don't get too excited. It's only about a million.

Ike (*his mouth drops open, astonished*)   What?! A million bucks! Pop?! That's impossible.

Monroe   I saw a Morgan Stanley statement.

Ike   He couldn't have saved that! He was a radio and TV repairman in a shit ass shop on East Main. How could he have earned a million bucks?

Monroe   He was like the personal radio and TV repairman to the Long Island mob families. He was socking it away.

Ike   I don't believe you. You're telling me he had megabucks when we were growing up?

Monroe   He must have.

Ike   Then why did he drive that broken-down Plymouth and live in that shitty little house? I didn't even have a room of my own.

Monroe   You had a room. I slept in the ruckus room most of the time. You're the only one he took on a vacation.

Ike   Just once to the Beaverkill River to fish for trout, but he was too cheap to stay overnight.

Monroe   He paid for Cory to go skiing.

Ike   I had to work two jobs just to get through Junior College.

Monroe   Jobs? Is that what you call 'em? You went to detention home for one of those jobs, Ike.

Ike   So when Pop pops off, we're like rich, right? A million bucks.

Monroe   Not if the nurse gets it.

Ike   We can contest the marriage.

Monroe   I've seen a lawyer. Even if he got married on his death bed, she could take it all.

Ike   That can't be true.

Monroe   The bastard charged me two grand to tell me that in New York children cannot challenge a marriage after the death of a parent.

Ike   God, if it ain't one thing . . . it's two things! There's a million bucks at stake here. This is serious.

Monroe   We've got to do something about her.

Ike (*making a rude gesture*)   I'm surprised you haven't tried.

Monroe   Who said I haven't?

The phone rings. **Monroe** *answers it.*

Monroe   Yes, Jean. She's here? Have her wait. No, never mind, send her in.

He hangs up.

Ike   What is it?

Monroe   Baby sister. Listen, don't say anything about how much money there is, okay.

Ike   Okay.

Monroe   I mean it, Ike!

Ike   I said okay.

Cory *enters.*

Cory   I'm going over to see Papa. I'm worried about him. Either of you want to come with me?

Monroe   No we don't. Why are you going? It's not Sunday.

Cory   Because this whole marriage thing is embarrassing and I think he's seriously depressed.

Monroe Nonsense. Sit down.

Ike *pulls up a chair for her and she sits.*

Monroe He's not mental, Cory. He's just trying to stir something up. He's doing it to spite me.

Ike How about me? He bailed me out once. That's the only good thing I can remember.

Cory We never missed a meal. We always had a roof over our heads. He paid for our education.

Monroe I got a scholarship.

Cory Yeah. Fifty bucks and a couple of free books. Who paid the rest? Just because he and Mother were always working is beside the point.

Ike I needed a father.

Cory It's not about you, it's about him! Papa's been married for almost forty-two years. He thinks he needs to still be married and he's grasping at the first straw – the nurse.

Monroe (*cynically to* **Ike**)   Our sister the analyst.

Cory I met a psychiatrist named Armand Nolan at a lecture. He thinks Papa may have a common condition in older people called 'amor dementia'. Brain scan images of people show that romantic love is a biological urge that knows no age limits.

Ike Bullshit. The nurse has her claws into our inheritance. She sees a vulnerable sick bastard with one foot in the grave and dollar signs are clanging in her eyes like fuckin' Daffy Duck.

Cory There won't be any money left when he dies, Ike. Franklin got free room and board as long as Mother donated her time at the home. Now it has to be paid for. And full care at the Manor costs seven thousand a month.

Ike No money left, eh?

Monroe   Shut up, Ike. Okay. Here's what we're gonna do. Dr Armand Nolan certifies that father's stroke has caused him to suffer diminished responsibility. That will give me the ammunition I need to go to court and petition to take over the estate as executor. He won't be able to marry without our consent.

Ike   I agree.

Cory   This is about helping Papa, right – figuring out how to get him through this without trauma or stress?

Monroe (*somewhat patronizingly*)   Yes, Cory. It's about helping Father come to his senses. Ike and I want him to be happy too. We need to spend more time with him. We should try to be a little more Catholic. Come here and give me a hug.

He approaches her. She avoids him.

Cory   Can I use your bathroom?

Monroe   Ask Jean for the key.

She exits.

Monroe   I think she's getting worse. Every time she touches someone she has to go wash her hands.

Ike   If she got laid she'd probably spend a month in the shower.

Monroe   Well, she may be nuts, but it's Father we've got to get certified insane.

Ike   What if he isn't?

Monroe   I've got ten thousand bucks I'll pay Dr Nolan to say he is. You can pay your share of that and the legal costs after we get what's coming to us.

Ike (*sarcastically*)   That's really big of you.

The lights fade.

Scene Four

The lights fade up on **Lester**'s *room at Bayside Manor. In the center of the room* **Lester** *reclines in his high-tech hospital bed. Upstage is a bookshelf containing* **Helen**'s *brass urn. The door to* **Lester**'s *room is closed. There is an empty breakfast tray on a trolly.* **Lily** *sits at the side of* **Lester**'s *bed with a copy of the New York Times unfolded.*

Lily (*reading*)   'Fifteen million Brazilians over the age of fourteen are illiterate. The director of the national library in Rio has quit because so many books had been eaten by termites.'

Lester   I had an uncle who was an entomologist with a huge collection of insects. He only had one leg and he used to tell us kids that his bugs ate the other one. I never found out the real reason.

Lily   Americans seem to know so little about their own relatives. In Japan we know everything.

Lester   I often think of things I never told my children.

Lily   For instance?

Lester   Well, it's a little thing, but when I was in the Navy my mates called me Prunzie.

Lily   Proonzie? What did they call you that?

Lester   On the first day of basic training they put a big bowl of prunes in front of me. I ate all of them.

Lily   What's wrong with that?

Lester   They were for the whole table!

Lily   You could have told your children.

Lester   They wouldn't have been interested.

Lily   Prune extract is a beauty product in Japan.

Lester   You don't say.

Lily   Ten million jars are sold each year.

Lester   No, really?

Lily   Six thousand Japanese citizens travel to California annually to see plum trees in bloom.

Lester   Well I'll be . . .

Lily   And to prune a tree means to encourage new growth.

Lester   I guess it does.

Lily   So I think prunes have made you a beautiful person open to growth.

Lester   I don't know what I would do without you, Lily.

There is a commotion outside the door and **Cory** *enters without knocking.* **Lily** *jumps to her feet and arranges the breakfast tray.*

Cory   Hi, it's me, Papa.

Lester   Don't you ever knock before you enter a room? I could have been indisposed.

Cory   Sorry, Papa. What are all those old women doing in the corridor?

Lester   They're waiting to read the paper to me. Especially that Mrs Gomez from the third floor with a shnozola like Durante.

Lily *gives a quizzical look.*

Lester   But I prefer Lily.

Lily *fusses around his bed straightening the blanket.*

Lily   Ogenki desu ka?

Lester   Genki desu, domo. (*To* **Cory**.) That means I'm fine, thanks.

Lily   Is there anything you need, darling?

Lester   Iie kekko desu. (*To* **Cory**.) That means, no thank you.

Lily   Are you finished with your breakfast?

Lester   Hai. (*To* **Cory**.) That means yes.

Lily   Did you eat everything?

Lester   Hai, my little geisha.

Lily   Another cup of coffee, my big kabuki warrior?

Lester   Iie kekko desu.

Lily   Shall I give you a bath now, or wait until your daughter has gone?

Lester   Come back in ten minutes.

Lily   Very well, Lester. Kiss, kiss.

Lester (*blowing kisses with his good right hand*)   Kiss, kiss. Sayonara. Ja matane. (*To* **Cory**.) That means see you later.

Lily *exits wheeling out the breakfast trolly.*

Cory   I think I'm going to puke!

Lester   Lighten up, Cory. You've got to start off each day with a song.

Cory   What's that? Another of your Japanese expressions?

Lester   No, Jimmy Durante.

Cory   I'm so worried about you, Papa.

Lester   Why?

Cory   What am I to think? Mama's only been in her grave . . . her urn . . . for a few weeks and you're behaving like a teenager.

Lester   No I'm not.

Cory   You have to wait the appropriate amount of time to marry again. You're grieving.

Lester   No I'm not.

Cory   You're depressed.

Lester   No I'm not.

Cory   You're in denial that Mother is dead.

Lester   No I'm not. She said she wanted me to be happy.

Cory   But this nurse is what? Thirty-two, thirty-three years younger than you!

Lester (*proudly*)   Thirty seven!

Cory   You're not in love with her.

Lester   How can you say that? I need her.

Cory   Why?

Lester   Who else is going to take care of me?

Cory   I could try.

Lester   You? You can't even stay out of the bathroom for five minutes. But there's one thing you can do for me.

Cory   What's that, Papa?

Lester   I want you to go see Franklin and tell him about his mother.

Cory   I know. I'll do it soon.

Lester   And take your brothers.

Cory   They won't come.

Lester (*agitated*)   I insist. I demand it. It's about time they started to obey me. You tell them.

Cory   Okay, Papa. Okay.

Lester (*beat*)   How are you really doing, Cory?

Cory   I'm okay, Papa.

Lester   Do you ever go skiing anymore?

Cory   Of course not, Papa.

Lester   Do you need any money?

Cory   I have all I need. I do really well on the Internet.

Lester   Are you trading . . . stocks?

Cory   I'm playing poker.

Lester   No.

Cory   Yes.

Lester   I thought gambling on the Internet was illegal.

Cory   It is. I simply applied for a credit card in England.

Lester   Have you always been this clever?

Cory   I think so, Papa. Last week I won nine grand.

Lester   That's amazing.

Cory   But I've got plenty of time on my hands. I could come over more, Papa. You don't need the nurse.

Lester   You couldn't handle the germs, Cory. Washing me. Feeding me? Not you.

Cory   I want you to see someone, Papa. I met him last week. His name is Armand and he likes me, Papa.

Lester (*nodding*)   I'm glad you've met 'someone'. Armand, eh?

Cory   He's going to a medical conference in Miami and I think he's going to invite me along. I think he could help you.

Lester   I don't need a shrink, Cory. I have all of my marbles. You go see Dr Gunther. He'll tell you I'm sharp as a tack.

Cory   I will see him, Papa, and I'm going to talk to the social worker too. We'll find a way to help you get through this. I can't bear to see you suffer.

Lester   Do whatever you want. You're as stubborn as I am.

Cory *exits* **Lester***'s room and comes downstage, pulling out her cellphone. She makes a call.*

Cory   Monroe Riley please. It's his sister, put him on now. (*Pause.*) Munny you've got to get over here after work. This is getting really bad. He won't listen. He's got an answer for everything. We've got to see Dr Gunther and get this sorted out. I mean it. Tonight. Try to find that little shit of a brother and bring him along too.

Back in **Lester***'s room,* **Helen***'s urn is lit. The two of them stand facing each other holding hands.*

Helen   I think you've upset her.

Lester   I shocked them all. An old dog can learn new tricks.

Helen   Tricks aren't love.

Lester   You gave *your* love to those poor kids in the home, but you didn't have enough left over for our own, did you?

Helen   Except Franklin. He has more love in him than the other three put together. Remember his poem? 'I love my daddee. He fixes radio and TV. He can fix anything, except for me . . .'

Both   '. . . except for me.'

Lester   He has a good heart and a sense of fun.

Helen   It's time for you to have some fun.

Lester   Lily helps.

Helen   She seems to care about you.

Lester   She's good to me.

Helen   You won't be dancing at your wedding.

Lester   I won't even be standing up at my wedding.

Helen   Remember our wedding waltz?

Music in: They start to dance the waltz.

Lester   We swept across the floor like Fred Astaire and Ginger Rogers.

Helen   Everyone applauded.

Lester   Even your father who hated me.

Helen   The world was our oyster.

Lester   I was the proudest man in New York.

Helen   We were so in love.

Lester   So carefree at twenty-three.

Helen   You got a loan to buy the shop.

Lester   Riley RadioVision Repairs.

Helen   We felt so rich.

Lester   Then the children arrived.

Helen   Monroe, Ike, Franklin . . .

Lester   Three boys in three years.

Helen   And Cory so much later. What a surprise!

Lester   An accident waiting to happen.

Helen   We tried to be good parents.

Lester   They weren't good children. (*Pause.*) I have a confession to make, Helen.

Helen   Yes, Lester?

Lester   I once made love to an underaged girl.

Helen (*mock shock*)   You dirty old man.

Lester   But I was only twelve at the time!

Helen   You were not twelve, you liar.

Lester   Why are you so sure?

Helen   Because it was me, dopey doo. We were both almost sixteen.

Lester   Well, how do you know you were the only one?

Helen (*knowing smile*)   I know. I know.

Lester's *face lights up in a smile as the lights dim.*

Scene Five

Lights come up on **Dr Gunther**'s *office. The doctor sits at his desk wearing a white lab coat.* **Monroe** *is looming above him, threateningly.* **Ike** *hovers in the background.*

Monroe   You're telling me that I can't hire a psychiatrist at my own expense to come in here . . . ?

Dr Gunther   If your idea is to get your father certified incapable of handling his own affairs, you will not be satisfied.

Monroe   Why not?

Dr Gunther   A few weeks ago, Lester asked me to call the noted psychiatrist Harold Goldstein from the Einstein College of Medicine. Goldstein gave him a clean bill of health. No dementia. No Alzheimer's. Completely of sound mind and compos mentis.

Monroe   He can't be. He wants to marry a twenty-something-year-old nurse!

Dr Gunther   That in and of itself does not constitute a symptom of dementia.

Monroe   I've a good mind to pull my father right the hell out of here, Doctor.

Dr Gunther   That won't be possible, Mr Riley. Your father has instructed the Peccorino firm of accountants to pay for his care here at Bayside Manor until the end of his lifetime, and to pay for Franklin's home.

Monroe   I'm his son. I can do whatever I want.

Dr Gunther   With all due respect, sir, I don't think so. His lawyers, Bobrow Haas and Partners, showed me a power of attorney over his financial and personal affairs, and a durable power of attorney for healthcare made out to *them*.

Monroe (*in shock*)   You're joking! He gave those shysters a power of . . . I . . . I . . . can't believe it!

Cory *barges in.*

Cory   Oh, you're here already? You could have at least waited for me to discuss our crazy father.

Monroe   Apparently he's not so crazy. He got himself certified sane by some quack at the Einstein College.

Ike   And he's given power of attorney to Bobrow Haas.

Cory   But we're his children.

Dr Gunther   Excuse me. Could the three of you take this outside. I have work to do.

Cory   Doctor, you're an understanding man. We have to get our father back. Don't the family's wishes count for anything?

Dr Gunther   Of course they do.

Cory   My brothers and I don't feel comfortable having our father treated by this particular nurse. Can we respectfully ask for her to be re-assigned?

Dr Gunther   No, Lester begged me to have Lily care for him. And our social worker doesn't see any reason why the relationship shouldn't continue.

Cory (*hopefully*)   But with your reference Lily could get a great job anywhere couldn't she?

Dr Gunther   Probably, yes. However, my opinion is that your father has come to terms with your mother's death. He is looking to the future. Where's the harm?

Cory (*tougher*)   The harm is, Doctor, that she is leading him on . . . she will break his heart.

Ike   Thirty-odd years age difference is not normal.

Monroe   The nurse doesn't care about him. She's obviously after his money. Why else would she be flirty with a stroke victim who has lost his marbles?

Dr Gunther (*amused*)   He's learning conversational Japanese, for goodness sake. Finding Lily gave him a spurt of energy. We were lucky to get her. She had offers from three other medical facilities.

Cory   But what does she see in him?

Dr Gunther   That's their business. But I have to tell you, Lily Hashimoto is one dedicated lady. We expect her to go to medical school one day.

Cory   So that's her game . . .

Monroe   Get my father to marry her and put her through medical school.

Ike   Get her a Green Card.

Dr Gunther   She already has one.

Ike (*mumbles*)   The old bastard is always one step ahead of us.

Cory   Please, Doctor, I don't want him to be hurt.

Monroe   I don't want him to be married.

Ike   I don't want him to screw us.

Dr Gunther   I think you should simply accept it. Give him your love and support and don't agitate him. Your father may be a relatively young stroke victim but he is not out of the woods.

Ike   You're saying he could have another one?

Dr Gunther   We can't be too careful. Now may I please ask you to let me go to work?

The lights fade on **Dr Gunther***'s office and up at the nurses' station downstage left.* **Lily** *is gathering bed linen.* **Monroe**, **Ike** *and* **Cory** *enter and confront her.*

Ike   Could we have a word with you, our future step-mother.

Lily   I promise I will not force you to eat your vegetables or brush your teeth.

Ike   Oh, she has a sense of humor too.

Monroe   C'mere. Gimme a hug.

Ike   Lay off it, Fossa.

Lily   What does this Fossa mean?

Ike   Just a little term of endearment I call my brother.

Monroe (*to* **Lily**)   You know, you're rather young to be carrying on with a man . . .

Lily (*interrupting*)   I am aware of my age.

Cory   Look, Lily. May I call you Lily?

Lily   That is my name.

Cory   Tell me where you come from?

Lily   I was born in Nagasaki.

Cory (*friendly*)   Was that a nice place to grow up?

Ike   For Chrissake, Cory, we bombed the shit out of 'em in the war . . .

Lily   I grew up not in Nagasaki but in Kobe, Japan and yes, nice could describe my upbringing.

Cory (*patronizingly*)   You seem a really intelligent girl. My brothers and I think it is not appropriate that our father enter into a relationship so soon after our mother's death. What do you think?

Lily   I do not judge Lester.

Ike   Well, young lady, Rester, as you call him, is not capable of making rational judgments at this time of his life.

Lily   I respectfully disagree. Your father is a stimulating, intelligent person despite his infirmity.

Cory   But surely you see that a marriage at his stage of life is ridiculous.

Lily   I see no such thing. He is still young. A stroke does not suddenly make one old. Why do you wish to stop his happiness?

Cory   We just don't want him to be hurt. Can't you understand that?

Lily *looks at her sympathetically and shrugs. A pregnant pause . . .*

Monroe   Look, let me ask you one thing. If this marriage goes ahead, would you be willing to sign an agreement about, you know . . .

Lily   No, I don't know.

Monroe   A pre-nup. Have you heard of a pre-nup?

Lily   Oh yes. Lester told me about them. (*Very rapidly.*) A pre-nuptial agreement is entered into when two people do not desire that their respective financial interests nor their real estate holdings be altered or changed by their marriage or civil union. They commonly include provisions for division of property in the event of divorce. Said agreement is binding upon both the parties and their successors under the state laws and statutes in which they reside, in this case the state of New York. Is that what you mean?

Monroe (*gulp*)   Uh, yes. That is what we mean.

Lily   I *will* sign any agreement . . .

Monroe   You will!?

Lily   Yes, I will . . .

Monroe (*relieved*)   Excellent . . .

Lily   . . . that Lester asks me to sign. And no agreement that any other person asks me to sign.

Monroe   But surely you see the logic in a family that wishes to keep the legal side of things, well, legal.

Lily   I wish everything to be legal.

Monroe   Look. You know that our father is Catholic. You're what? Buddhist? Shinto?

Lily (*pause*)   I am Catholic.

Shock and surprise.

Ike   This gets worse and worse.

Cory   Now, Lily. You're a young woman. A smart woman. You'll want to travel the world and he is stuck here for the rest of his life.

Monroe   Let me handle this. (*To* **Lily**.) Look here. What would it cost for you to go away?

Lily   What do you mean?

Monroe   How many thousand dollars would you need to move to another city and find another job?

Lily   I will not. This is my place of work. My life is here. I want to be with your father.

Cory   Surely you don't love him.

Lily   If he loves me, I love him. And may I tell you a Japanese proverb you should take to heart: 'Take care of your parents while they are still alive. You cannot help them from beyond the grave.'

Monroe   What the hell's that supposed to mean?

Lily   Excuse me. I must see to your father. It is his bedtime.

Ike   I need a drink.

Cory   They have wine in the cafeteria.

Monroe   We need to talk.

The lights fade on the nurses' station and up again on **Lester***'s room.*

Scene Six

Lily *enters* **Lester***'s room carrying fresh bed linen which she places on a chair next to the bed.*

Lily   It's time to make your bed, Lester. Can we move you to the wheelchair?

Lester   I'm a little tired, Lily, and my leg hurts.

Lily   Then I'll just make the bed with you in it.

Lester   Oh boy!

Lily   I'm going to try for the world speed record.

Lester   Okay.

Lily   Start your clocks. Ready, get set . . . go!

Lily *springs into action. At a bound, she raises the side rails on the stage right side of the bed. Then she pushes* **Lester** *onto his side and he hangs on to the rail. She loosens the bottom sheet at the head and foot and rolls the bottom sheet and blanket close to* **Lester***'s back. She lays down the new clean fitted bottom sheet folded lengthwise from head to foot ends of the bed and tucks them in and smoothes out the sheet. She rolls the remaining bottom sheet lengthwise close to* **Lester***'s back so it is right beside the old bottom sheet.*

Lily   Okay, Lester. Rock and roll towards me over the sheets.

He does so, laughing. She raises the stage left side rail and **Lester** *grabs hold of it. She moves to the other side of the bed, loosens the old bottom sheet and pulls it completely off the bed as well as pulling the new sheet from under* **Lester***. She tucks in the new bottom sheet at*

the head and foot of the bed and smoothes out the wrinkles. She rolls
Lester *back to the center of the bed. Racing against the clock she*
replaces the old pillowcases. She throws a blanket over him and she
places a clean sheet on top of the blanket.

Lily   Grab hold of the blanket and sheet, Lester.

She pulls the old top sheet from the foot of the bed onto the floor, and
then turns the new top sheet and blanket around so the blanket is on
top. She tucks the top sheet, blankets and throws on the bed spread.
She then puts her hands in the air like she has won the marathon.

Lily   How was it for you?

Lester   Fabulous. It's a new world's record.

Lily   Next year we must enter the Olympics!

Lester   Whew! I think I need a rest.

Lily   I could do it again!

Lester   Domo, my little lotus blossom.

She douses the lights.

Lester   My leg feels strange. (*Sexy.*) How about a little leg
massage?

Lily   Where does it hurt?

Lester   Just above the knee.

Lily   It may be your vastus medialus, the muscle in your
lower quad.

Cory, **Monroe** and **Ike** *appear in the corridor outside* **Lester***'s*
room.

Cory   We'll just talk it out calmly and lovingly like the
supportive children that we are. And don't get hot tempered
and demand that he stop seeing her.

Ike   Why the hell not?

Cory   He's stubborn. It'll make him want her more.

Monroe   Okay, maybe you're right. We'll handle this calmly. Like adults.

Cory   Good. Cool.

Monroe, **Ike** *and* **Cory** *enter the darkened room. They see the dimly lit form of* **Lily** *moving over* **Lester**.

Monroe   What the . . .

Ike   Fuck!

Cory   Papa?!

The lights come on suddenly. **Lester***'s high-tech bed is in the upright position and his bare legs are propped up and spread wide.* **Lily** *faces the bed upstage, her head between* **Lester***'s legs, the blanket covering her head. The 'children' view her little lace panties. To them she appears to be giving* **Lester** *a . . .*

Cory   What are you doing?

Lester   Hi, kids!

Blackout. Curtain. End of Act One.

Act Two

Scene One

Lester's *room at the Manor. He is sitting up in bed.* **Lily** *sits in a chair next to the bed holding the science section of the New York Times.*

Lily   Oh. This is surprising. Here is an article about an endangered mammal I have never heard of.

Lester   Which one?

Lily   Let me read it to you. 'The male *fossa*, dubbed the Pink Panther of Madagascar, has the largest penis bone of all the cat-like species. The adult *fossa* is about three and a half feet long and has a penis of about seven inches.'

Lester   Did you say *fossa*?

Lily   Yes, isn't that what your younger son calls his brother?

Lester (*roaring with laughter*)   Oh my God. All these years Ike has been calling Munny a big prick.

A knock and **Barry Gillis** *appears at the door carrying a bunch of sunflowers.*

Barry   Hola, Lester. Long time no see. I brought you these from your garden.

Lester   But we don't live there anymore.

Barry   I know but they were hanging over my fence.

Lester   Come on in, Barry. I'm glad you got my message.

Barry   It sounded urgent.

Lily   I'll put those in water and leave you to visit.

She takes sunflowers from **Barry** *and exits.*

Lester   Sayonara, Lily.

Barry   Adios, Lily.

Lily *exits.* **Barry** *sits down in the chair she has vacated.*

Lester   Do you know what a fossa is, Barry?

Barry   What Ike calls Munny? No I don't.

Lester   A cat with a big dick. Ha!

Barry   My my. You learn something new every day. So all these years Ike's been calling his brother . . . a cat?

Lester   Something like that.

Barry   I just ran into them.

Lester   Who?

Barry   Your children.

Lester   Where?

Barry   Here. All of them, well except Franklin, of course. They're outside talking in the garden.

Lester   Interesting. What are they up to?

Barry   Don't know. Lurking around.

Lester   Anything new in the old neighborhood?

Barry   The house on the other side of yours sold for three hundred and seventy-nine grand.

Lester   Not bad in this economy.

Barry   I don't want to go but maybe I should sell too.

Lester   You built that house with your own two hands.

Barry   Yeah, but it's too big for me now since Elaine passed, and Tommy never comes around. Maybe I'll move here.

Lester   It's a good place. There are lots of women.

Barry   Women? I couldn't care less.

Lester   You might like it. I hear talk about wild nights on the third floor with a certain Mrs Gomez and a bunch of geriatric dancers.

Barry   Well, I'll be a monkey's uncle.

Lester   Barry, I wanted to see you in person to ask you a favor.

Barry   What is it?

Lester   I want you to be my best man.

Barry (*moved*)   Are you sure? You want me?

Lester   I'm sure, my friend.

Barry   No problemo, Lester, I will do it con mucho gusto and I'm honored. But are you sure you're doing the right thing?

Lester   My mind is made up. And I want you to buy me the ring. I can't give Lily Helen's ring. I'll leave that to Cory. But if you could go down to East Main and see a jeweler there named Henry Kleiman. Tell him to make me something in the ten thousand dollar neighborhood.

Barry   Wow! That's a nice neighborhood. You sure you can spend that much dinero, y'know – cash on the barrelhead?

Lester   Yep. Tell him to send the bill to my accountants Peccorino.

Barry (*rising to go*)   Will do. Adios amigo . . .

Lester   Oh Barry, one more thing.

Barry   Yes, Lester.

Lester   What's the name of that skinny kid down the street who became a travel agent?

Barry   Westerman? The kid with the heebie jeebies?

Lester   Yeah, that's him. Do me a favor and look him up.

Barry   Why? He sells high-priced luxury vacations.

Lester   I'm in the market.

Barry (*suddenly realizes*)   What? Are you out of your cotton-pickin' mind? You're going on a honeymoon – in your condition?

Lester (*shrugs*)   Why not?

Barry (*starts to exit shaking his head in wonder*)   Okay! Hasta la vista, Lester.

Lester   Domo, Barry, and when you see my children on the way out, be sure to tell them about the ring.

Barry   Yo comprendo, Lester.

Lester   Arigato gozaimahsu.

The lights fade and the light comes up on **Helen***'s urn. She materializes in the room.*

Lester   Helen? Are you here?

Helen   Yes, dear.

Lester (*rising*)   Do you believe our children are visiting again?

Helen   You've stirred them up.

Lester   Maybe I should have done more of that when they were young.

Helen   You did your best, but you weren't generous.

Lester   I scrimped and saved every cent for our old age. And you go and die on me before I could give it to you.

Helen   That's life.

Lester   And I never told you how much we had.

Helen   I wouldn't have cared.

Lester (*sadly*)   I often dreamed I could be on a tropical beach with you singing 'It's a long long time from May to December . . .'

Helen   You waited too long for our September Song, Lester.

Lester   I should have taken you to Paris, Venice, Rome.

Helen   I would have liked that.

Lester   I always wanted to see the pyramids . . .

Helen   You never told me.

Lester   They were too far away from my shop on East Main.

Helen   Too late now.

Lester   No, it's not. It's not too late for me to make it up to you. I know the way. I'll show you. You'll be proud of me.

Helen   I've always been proud of you. That's why our marriage was a success. Three rules.

Lester   Never go to bed mad.

Helen   Always have a sense of humour.

Lester   Separate toilets.

A knock at the door. **Helen** *evaporates,* **Lester** *slithers into his bed, and the lights on the urn fade.*

Lester   Come in.

Cory, **Monroe** *and* **Ike** *enter.*

Monroe (*earnestly*)   Father. We're all here to see you. Ike and Cory and me.

Lester   Louder, I can't hear you. Ike, get my hearing aid in the drawer. It's wrapped in some paper.

Ike *rummages in the drawer of the bedside table and finds the hearing aid wrapped in a bank statement. He glances at the bank statement in astonishment and stuffs it in his pocket.*

Lester   What are you waiting for?

Ike *puts the hearing aid into his father's left ear and adjusts the power pack.*

Ike   Can you hear us now? Di di dit, dah dah dah, di di dit.

Lester   That's Morse Code for SOS. I learned it when I was a kid building crystal set radios.

Ike (*to himself*)   Code? I never knew . . .

Lester   Did you know that Thomas Edison proposed to his wife in Morse Code?

Ike *is quite agitated. During this scene he glances a few times at the bank statement, not believing his eyes.*

Cory   We're all concerned about you, Papa.

Lester   Thanks, but don't be.

Cory   We went to see Franklin yesterday, Papa.

Lester   The three of you?

Monroe   Yes, Father.

Lester   That's good. Well done, Cory. Did you tell him about Mother?

Monroe   Yes, he cried.

Cory   He hugged us, Papa.

Lester (*surprised*)   You let him touch you, Cory?

Cory   Yes I did, Papa. He even hugged Ike!

Lester   Why wouldn't he?

Ike   I uh, hit him once, Pop, it was an accident . . . I . . .

Lester   I'm glad you told him.

Cory   We all cried, Papa. Look. He made you a card. Drew it himself.

Cory *takes a large greeting card out of her handbag and hands it to* **Lester**. **Lester** *looks at the card holding it with his good right hand right up against his right eye. After a pause:*

Lester (*reading card*)   'To my daddy Lester Riley. My heart goes out to you.' My God. He must have signed his name thirty-five times!

Monroe   We have a suggestion to make, Father. Before you marry Lily, can we write an appropriate legal document between the two of you?

Lester   Why?

Monroe   Because it's sensible at your time of life to have a pre-nuptial agreement.

Lester   Why?

Monroe   Because it protects you and her.

Lester   From what?

Monroe   Well, face it, Father. You aren't going to live forever.

Lester   I know. But I don't want any pre-nuptial agreement.

Monroe (*patiently*)   But what if you die and leave your money to Lily and then, God forbid, what if she dies? Then all your money is going to go to some people in Nagasaki or Hiroshima or some God-forsaken place – people you've never even met. Now me and Ike and Cory, we're your family. Do you think that would be fair?

Lester   My money won't go to people in Japan, Munny.

Monroe   How can you be so sure?

Lester   Because if Lily died then all her money would be inherited by . . . her little son.

Monroe   Son?

Ike   Son?!

Cory   She's got a son?!

Lester   Yes! You are going to have a step-brother!

Monroe   But Father, how can you think you could possibly be a father to him?

Lester   I'll worry about that next Saturday.

Cory   Saturday?

Ike   What the hell is happening next Saturday?

Lester   Saturday Lily will begin living the wife of Riley. Get it?

Monroe (*confused*)   What did he say?

Lester   The wedding! Next Saturday. St Hugh's! We're getting married!

Blackout. SFX – a huge thunderclap. Rain and thunderstorm FX in under:

Scene Two

A dim light comes on downstage right. **Father Riordan** *sits reading, a candle on the table.* **Cory**, **Monroe** *and* **Ike** *enter shaking the rain off their raincoats.*

Father Riordan   Ah, the Riley clan. Come in. Is your father alright?

Monroe   Yes, he's fine.

Father Riordan   What brings you out on a terrible night like this?

Cory   We had to see you urgently, Father. It's about the wedding.

Father Riordan   Everything's all set for Saturday at ten.

Cory   Father, don't you really think that Papa is behaving foolishly with such a young woman?

Father Riordan   Everyone needs someone.

Cory   Can I ask if you have spent any time with him about this marriage business?

Father Riordan   Yes, I have. We've discussed it thoroughly.

Cory   But Father, isn't it true that to be married in the church a bride and groom must undergo extensive marriage counseling?

Father Riordan   Yes, forty-five hours-worth. Almost fifteen percent of the couples postpone their marriage and eight percent cancel the wedding completely.

Cory   And have you actually given any of your marriage counseling guidance to Papa and that nurse?

Father Riordan   Well to be honest, I didn't deem that to be entirely necessary, Corinne.

Cory   Why should they be treated differently?

Father Riordan   I figure it this way. Your father was successfully and faithfully married for forty-two years. He's one of the most experienced bridegrooms I've ever met!

Cory   How about twenty hours of counseling over two months?

Father Riordan   Not necessary, dear.

Cory   Okay, Father, I didn't want to bring this up, but are you aware that Lily has an illegitimate child? You can't marry her in the church.

Father Riordan   Where did you get that idea, Corinne? Mrs Hashimoto is a widow.

Cory   Mrs?!

Monroe   A widow!

Ike   Fuck!

Father Riordan   I'll see you Saturday at ten at the wedding. Don't be late!

Father Riordan's *light fades. The three of them close the door and pause outside.*

Monroe   We're screwed.

Ike   We sure are, you fuckin' liar.

Monroe   What do you mean?

Ike   You're a liar and you're a thief.

Cory   Stop it, Ike, you're in a church. What's got into you?

Ike   Munny told me Pop had about a million dollars. He told me he saw a bank statement.

Cory   A million dollars? That's impossible. (*To* **Monroe**.) You never told me that!

Ike (*brandishing the bank statement*)   This proves it.

Cory   What is it?

Ike   It's a Morgan Stanley bank statement I found wrapped around his hearing aid. It says he's worth two point three million! Our fuckin' brother was going to steal the rest.

Blackout.

Scene Three

Monroe's *home. The storm continues outside with thunder and lightning.* **Monroe**, **Cory** *and* **Ike** *drag themselves inside.* **Monroe** *turns on the lights which crackle and pop with electricity.*

Monroe   Don't leak water on the carpet, Ike. Throw your coats in the hall bathroom.

Cory   I didn't know you lived so close to St Hugh's.

Monroe   We moved here just after I stopped going. Ironic, eh?

Ike   Nice house. Big.

Monroe   You've been here before.

Ike   You never invited me.

Cory   Or me.

Monroe   I was sure you'd been here . . . say, are you hungry? I could make some scrambled eggs.

Cory   No, we're not hungry. Let's get down to business. I've got to get home before it gets any worse.

Ike (*heated*)   Why did you say the estate was worth a million when it's worth two point three?

Cory (*agitated*)   And why did you tell Ike and not me? I don't care about the money. I care about you treating me my whole life like I wasn't there.

Ike   Well, I do care about the money. I want what's coming to me. Were you ever gonna tell us the truth?

Monroe (*slickly*)   Look. I swear to you it was only a million when I saw the papers. I would have told you after I got all the books and figured out the Manor and Franklin's expenses at the home. I wouldn't lie to you. Anyway, it doesn't make a damn bit of difference if that nurse gets it.

Ike   Two point three mil makes one hell of a difference . . . (*Viciously.*) Fossa!

Cory   Okay, let's calm down and discuss this like rational human beings for a change.

Ike   How can we be rational when that nurse is fucking him and fucking us too?

Cory   What right do we have to claim father's estate – just because we were born?

Ike   Yes, we're his children! It's our birthright!

Cory   Nonsense. If we were truly concerned about Papa's wellbeing we would give our blessing to his marriage. He's a grown man.

Ike   You're a fuckin' lunatic.

Cory   Stop making allusions to my mental state, Ike.

Ike (*lashing back*)   You can't even stay married for five minutes.

Monroe   That's outa line, Ike.

Cory (*emotional*)   My husband died in a skiing accident and you know it.

Monroe   Stop it both of you. We only have a week to figure out what to do about this marriage. There has to be something we haven't thought of.

Ike   Kidnap the nurse?

Cory   Let's be sensible.

Ike   I'm being sensible.

Cory   Why is your first reaction always criminal, Ike? All your life you sucked up to the families down the street doing their little errands for them.

Ike   They respected me.

Cory   They used you. You know why you got caught robbing the airline payroll? Because the mob guys sold you out.

Ike   Oh yeah? When my good pal Gianni Santangelo gets out of Elmira you'll see the respect I get.

Cory   Your good friend Gianni was probably the one who called the cops on you.

Ike   Why don't you fuck off skiing!

Cory *bursts into tears.* **Ike** *plops down in an armchair and shrugs, wondering if maybe she's right about Gianni. A huge stroke of lightning strikes outside and the lights in* **Monroe**'s *house start flickering.*

Monroe I think we're in for it. (*To* **Cory**.) I really want you to stay here tonight, Cory. There's no getting home in this weather. Please?

Cory (*agitated*) I'm not comfortable.

Monroe Give it a chance. We've got to get this sorted out tonight.

Cory Call me a taxi.

Monroe You'll never get one.

Cory I can't sleep in your house. I've got a routine.

Monroe (*patiently*) Your routine needs to be put on hold, Cory.

Cory I need to go to the bathroom again. Where – Is – It? Now!

Monroe (*sympathetically*) Let's try to deal with this, Cory. Calm down. You can do it. What about this psychiatrist friend of yours? What's his name?

Cory Armand.

Monroe (*paternally*) Why don't you give him a call? If he can't help you stay here, I'll drive you home myself, blizzard or not.

Cory I'll try, Munny . . .

Monroe Good girl. Use the phone in the guest room, sweetheart. It's the first room up the stairs. Talk as long as you like.

Cory Munny?

Monroe Yeah?

Cory Did you just call me . . . sweetheart?

Monroe Christ, did I? I must be going soft.

Cory *exits.* **Ike** *paces up and down the living room.*

Ike (*agitatedly*)   Fossa, we've got to do something. There's gotta be a way to stop this thing.

Monroe   We've tried everything – the legal, the psychiatric, the religious. I tried to buy her off. What else is there?

Ike   He's had one bad stroke. He could go anytime.

Monroe   What? What are you saying? He's your father.

Ike (*distraught*)   A lot of things can stop a wedding, Fossa. The bride could disappear, the priest could get called away on an emergency, there could be a fire, somebody could have a freak accident. Records could go missing . . .

Monroe (*horrified*)   You're not talking about actually hurting him . . . ?

Ike   Accidents happen.

Monroe   I won't condone violence.

Ike   Since when?! You beat the shit out of me half our life, even in front of our friends at Mother's memorial.

Monroe   Now listen to me . . .

Ike   No, I won't. You've always kept me down. You could've helped me but you never did. This time you're not going to stand in my way.

Monroe   He's your father, Ike.

Ike   Yeah and he's giving that nurse a ten thousand dollar fuckin' wedding ring! You know what's the matter with you? You're a spineless, thieving, incompetent lying prick. No wonder Pop wouldn't show you the books.

Monroe   C'mon, Ike, listen to reason. We can work this out.

Ike (*determined*)   Something's going to happen, Fossa. I know some people – people who respect family values and traditions – people who can help me keep what is mine – a big chunk of two point three million bucks – and I'm gonna go see them. I'm going to tell them everything, and they're gonna listen, and then we're going to do something about it!

Monroe Come to your senses, man . . .

Ike I am going out and get what's mine!

Monroe Don't be stupid . . . I can help . . . I promise . . .
Ike . . . please . . . !

Ike *stomps off and slams the front door, echoed by a thunderclap.
The lights come up on* **Cory** *in a bedroom at* **Monroe**'s *house. The
storm SFX continue.* **Cory** *sits on a couch. She is shaking, almost
uncontrollably.* **Monroe** *enters hurriedly, distraught.*

Monroe We've got to do something, Cory. Ike's going off
the deep end. We've got to go after him. Cory . . .

She stares catatonically into space.

Cory, what's wrong? Are you okay?

Cory (*despair*) He wasn't there.

Monroe Who?

Cory Armand. I left a message. He went to Miami for a
week . . . alone.

Monroe It'll be alright.

Cory No it won't. You don't know anything.

Monroe I could uh, maybe try to help you, Cory.

Cory I doubt it.

Monroe The storm will pass . . .

Cory I'm not afraid of storms, but I need to be in my
own place.

Monroe Take the guest room upstairs. There's a great bed.

Cory (*angry*) I can't sleep in someone else's bed. I'll rest
here on the couch.

Monroe How did it come to this, Cory?

Cory I don't know. It's just the way I am.

Monroe   When did it start? Tell me about it.

Cory   Way back . . . a long time.

Monroe   You want me to play you some music?

Cory   You have any Leonard Cohen?

Monroe   God, no. I've got a DeCastro Sisters CD somewhere.

Cory   Forget it.

Monroe   You want me to read you a bedtime story?

Cory   Don't be stupid.

Monroe   Why don't you tell *me* a story. I'm a good listener.

Cory   Since when?

Monroe   I dunno, maybe today.

Cory   I'm no good at stories.

Monroe   Tell me about a little girl and something that made her unhappy.

Cory   You wouldn't like it.

Monroe   Try me. Once upon a time . . .

Cory   You don't want to hear this.

Monroe   Please? Once upon a time . . .

A long pause, and then . . .

Cory (*completely monotone*)   Once upon a time there was a little girl whose parents were seldom at home. She looked up to her two older brothers and hoped they would be nice to her. One afternoon she came home from school and made herself a peanut butter and jelly sandwich. She heard noises from the ruckus room. She went downstairs and opened the door a crack. She saw her oldest brother standing naked in front of a disgusting girl from down the street and he was taking off her bra. He had an erection and pubic hair which the little girl had never seen before.

Monroe   Oh, Cory. Oh, my.

Cory   Her other brother and Tommy from next door were tearing the clothes off another neighbor girl. She closed the door and ran up the stairs and went to her room and locked the door and thought she could never be the same with her brothers again. She would never again hug or touch them because they might do something . . . awful to her. So she avoided them whenever she could. And she never felt really clean.

Monroe (*mortified*)   Oh, dear, oh, dear. I'm so . . . sorry.

Cory   I'm sorry too. And I'm sad that the little girl was so frightened of them for all those years and avoided them just because they were doing what boys do.

Monroe   We hurt you. I never realized.

Cory   You weren't the only ones . . .

Monroe   Oh, dear me. I've been meaning to give you something.

Monroe *fumbles in his pocket and pulls out a hundred dollar bill and offers it to her.*

Take this.

Cory   What's is it?

Monroe   The ten bucks I lost on that bet at Barry's. With interest.

Cory (*ironic laugh*)   As Papa would probably say, 'Forget the money, Munny.'

The lights fade and up on **Lily** *pushing* **Lester** *in his wheelchair in the garden of Bayside Manor. Suddenly . . .*

Lily   Here comes the dance of the wheelchair.

Music in: Jimmy Durante's 'Hi-Lily, Hi Lo.' **Lily** *manipulates the wheelchair in a choreographed dance, swooping* **Lester** *across the stage. The wheelchair takes off without her and she has to run after* *it and catch it before* **Lester** *plunges into the audience.* **Lester** *is laughing merrily.*

Lester   That's about as close as we're going to get to a wedding dance, Lily. I hope you don't mind.

Lily   I wish your children could see how happy you are.

Lester   I think they are more worried about their own happiness. They have learned some things about me recently they didn't know before.

Lily   What things?

Lester   I left a paper for Ike to find. They have discovered I am a man of certain means. Maybe I've gone too far. But it's too late to stop it now.

The lights fade on **Lester** *and* **Lily** *and up on* **Monroe** *and* **Cory**. *They are sitting at a bar with cognacs in front of them. It's late at night.*

Cory   Two days and not a sign of him.

Monroe   I don't know where else to look. He's going to do something really stupid. I can feel it.

Cory   He wouldn't hurt anybody, would he? Has he ever . . . hurt somebody?

Monroe   I don't know. He once carried a gun.

Cory   Did you try that Italian club on East Pulaski?

Monroe   Yeah. Theresa Scalise's brother Frankie was there. They haven't seen him.

Cory   And we don't know where he was working.

Monroe   All he told me was he was making ends meet. He said he worked out. I tried every gym in town.

Cory   What are we going to do?

Monroe   I don't know. I feel so helpless I can't even find my own brother.

Cory (*starting to cry*)   Me too. We never found each other. Our whole lives.

Monroe   Maybe we didn't look hard enough.

Cory   Maybe it's not too late.

Monroe   I'm sorry too, sweetheart. We've got to stick together. Okay?

Cory   Okay.

Monroe   Do you need any money?

Cory   Nope.

Monroe   Can I hug you?

Cory   No.

Monroe   You want to spend the night again at my house?

Cory   Okay.

Scene Four

Fade up on the study of **Ettore Santangelo**'*s mansion.* **Ike** *is pacing up and down, extremely nervously. He looks at pictures hanging on the walls and begins to hyperventilate. He is about to run for the door when* **Santangelo** *enters. He is a distinguished-looking businessman in a suit and tie with a shock of steely grey hair. He looks at* **Ike** *for an uncomfortable minute.*

Santangelo   My son Gianni sent a message from inside you wanted to see me.

Santangelo *sits in an armchair.* **Ike** *stands nervously in front of him.*

Ike   Yeah. We became really close friends at Elmira.

Santangelo   He tells me you once had a fight.

Ike   When we were kids.

Santangelo   Put you in the hospital . . .

Ike   Mild concussion. Scrambled my brains a bit. Heh, heh.

Santangelo (*not finding that funny*)   He was a good fighter. Could have turned pro if he was smarter.

Ike   I'm sure he could've.

Santangelo   Here's a kid who did some serious shit and what did they get him for? Rape. Unbelievable this legal system.

Ike   It was bad luck.

Santangelo   The Scalises paid. So what can I do for you?

Ike   I know how much you honor . . . family . . . tradition . . . being fair . . . punishing wrong. It's uh, hard to explain. My uh . . . it's like this . . . you see . . .

Ike *sputters and strains to find the words.*

Santangelo   Take it easy. Deep breath.

Ike   We grew up down the street . . .

Santangelo   Which house? What's your last name again?

Ike   Riley.

Santangelo   Your father wasn't the TV man was he?

Ike   Yeah.

Santangelo (*serious*)   Not Lester Riley?

Ike (*apprehensive*)   Yeah . . .

Santangelo (*a smile spreads across his face*)   Lester Riley! He was a real friend to our family. You've got one hellova father, kid. Help yourself to a drink.

Ike *goes over to a table with drinks and nervously pours himself a huge whiskey from an ornate cut glass decanter.*

Santangelo   I heard he had a stroke. How's he doing?

Ike (*surprised*)   Yes, he's uh, doing okay. My mother died.

Santangelo   Oh, I'm sorry. Helen was quite a woman. We go way back, your old man and my family.

Ike   You do?

Santangelo   I was one of his first customers. One day my mother, God rest her soul, was listening to her big Zenith radio and there was a little puff of smoke and the thing dies. She calls me up. 'Ettore, you gotta getta this a radio fixed for me right away.' I remember seeing a new sign going up over on East Main – Riley RadioVision Repairs. So my pal Fat Mike Calabrase and me put the radio in the car and run it over there. We meet this young kid who owns the shop – your old man. He puts the old Zenith on the bench, unscrews the back, and takes off the back panel. There's a horrible stench – and a huge dead rat falls out!

Ike   A rat?!

Santangelo (*laughing*)   It was completely fried! Fat Mike is holding his nose. I'm laughing my ass off. Your father picks up the rat by its ears and says 'I didn't know you people were into electrocution'. He was a real joker your old man. But he was serious when it counted. We always used to seek out his advice.

Ike   You mean on what TVs and radios to buy?

Santangelo   Naw, not just that. On all kinds of things. I wouldn't be the businessman I am today if it wasn't for your father.

Ike (*incredulous*)   You wouldn't?

Santangelo   He set up a little investment syndicate. He called it the Zenith Fund after my mother's rat radio. I socked some money into it and did very well. We all did. He was a real smart guy with money.

Ike   You're joking.

Santangelo (*dead serious*)   I don't joke, kid.

Ike   Sorry.

Santangelo   And there was that one time when he really saved our life.

Ike   When was that?

Santangelo   What? Your old man never told you about the Super Bowl?

Ike   No.

Santangelo   I can't believe he never told you. It wasn't called the Super Bowl yet – just the AFL-NFL World Championship Game – second Sunday in January '67. About twelve-thirty my relatives show up and Eddie Scalise, who was a friend in those days, brings his cousins, and some Gambino guys drop around. They all brought beer and food. It was quite a party. I had this twenty-four inch top-of-the-line RCA your father got me wholesale. The pre-game program was broadcast on two channels so we're switchin' back and forth from Ray Scott and Frank Gifford on CBS to Curt Gowdy on NBC. Suddenly the set fades out to a little dot in the middle of the screen. We check the power cord and try every button but nothin' works. Now it's one and we're panicked 'cause the game starts at two. We have to watch that game! In that room there is probably something like sixty grand in bets laid out. So we send Tony Indelicato down to your house to bring your father.

Ike   He was home? He usually went right to the shop after church.

Santangelo   You're right, he must have been in the shop 'cause he had all his tools with him. Anyway, Good Lookin' Tony breaks all the speed limits and Lester arrives and takes off the back panel. 'I can't fix this today,' he says, 'the rectifier tube is burned out. The wholesale house is closed on Sunday.' Somebody, I think it was Artie Calabrase, says, 'Where's the fuckin' wholesale house? We'll break in.' So three or four of the boys drag your father into the car, rush over to the joint, jimmy the lock, and take the tubes and stuff. Lester insists the boys leave cash on the register. Then they race back here, and he starts to work. He's pulling out wires and tubes and his soldering iron was smokin'. Finally the set comes back to life just in time to see Max McGee catch Bart Starr's pass for the first touchdown. The boys pick up your father, put him on their shoulders and march him around the room like *he* had scored the touchdown. The Green Bay Packers beat the Kansas City Chiefs 35–10. I win eighty-five hundred bucks. After that we made sure your old man got all our business. We probably bought a thousand TVs from him.

Ike   He never told us.

Santangelo   Some of the boys had a trophy made up special for him like a bowling trophy. Did you ever see it?

Ike   No.

Santangelo   You gotta ask him about it. You're gonna die!

He hits **Ike** *on the back and* **Ike** *nearly drops his drink.*

Ike (*dryly*)   I can't wait.

Santangelo   He's a modest man, your father. Now what was it that you wanted?

Ike   Oh, it's nothing.

Santangelo   You can ask me anything, kid.

Ike   My father . . . my father . . .

Santangelo   Yeah?

Ike (*brightly*)   . . . is getting married again.

Santangelo (*suspicious*)   That's what you came to tell me?

Ike   The bride is his nurse.

Santangelo   So?

Ike   She's a pretty young Japanese girl.

Santangelo (*amused*)   I'm glad he's feeling up to it.

Ike (*defeated*)   Yeah, well. He uh . . . he just wanted your blessing . . .

Santangelo (*serious, dangerous*)   Oh, now I get it – why you wanted to see me. You're unhappy with this situation and you thought I might . . . get involved. Well I'll tell you three things, kid. One – we never meddle in affairs of the heart. Two – we only take care of our own. And three – we've burned all our bridges. Tell your old man.

Ike   He'll know what that means?

Santangelo   We're on hundred per cent legit now. All the 'old' businesses have been sold to the other families.

Lights fade.

Scene Five

Lester's *room at the Manor. It is late at night and he is asleep.* **Cory** *enters and drags a chair up to his bed. She sits fidgeting.* **Lester** *stirs.*

Lester   Lily?

Cory   No, it's me, Papa.

Lester   Cory? What time is it?

Cory   Almost midnight, Papa.

Lester   What day is it?

Cory   It'll soon be Wednesday. Three days to go. Papa, we're worried about Ike.

Lester   Who's worried?

Cory   Munny and me.

Lester Munny and you together? You're worried about your brother?

Cory He's been gone a few days. We tried to find him, but we can't.

Lester Oh, he'll turn up. Like a bad Indian Head penny.

Cory We're afraid he may try to do something to stop your wedding.

Lester Oh, I don't think there's anything to be concerned about. Are you here alone?

Cory Someone drove me.

Lester Did you make any money this week playing poker?

Cory Four thousand.

Lester Did I ever tell you when I was in the Navy they called me Prunzie?

Cory No, Papa.

Lester Don't you want to ask me why?

Cory Because you liked prunes?

Lester Yeah. I guess so. You were always my favorite, Cory.

Cory I know, Papa. But we didn't see that much of each other.

Lester We gave you freedom. We didn't stop you from going to that hippy nudist place.

Cory Maybe you should've. I was only nineteen. I can't believe I got pregnant the first time I ever did it with a guy.

Lester Your mother was mad about the abortion.

Cory She didn't talk to me for years.

Lester Did we talk?

Cory I called you once at the shop.

Lester   Was I there?

Cory   You were always there. But you said you had a customer and would call me back.

Lester (*guiltily*)   I didn't do it, did I?

Cory   No. You were ashamed of me.

Lester   I have so many regrets.

Cory   Me too.

Lester   I caused you pain.

Cory   You thought you were doing the right thing.

Lester   We were there for the most important things, weren't we?

Cory   I guess so, Papa. Yesterday I went to St Hugh's to pray for Mother.

Lester   You forgive her, that's good.

Cory (*after a pause*)   I want you to know something.

Lester   What's that?

Cory   You can marry her. Lily.

Lester   I can?

Cory   You don't need my permission, of course, but I accept that if this is something that can bring joy and contentment at your time of life, you must do it.

Lester   Domo, Cory. I was hoping for your blessing. You know what I wish?

Cory   What's that?

Lester   That you take charge of your demons.

Cory   I'm getting better, Papa. I've even slept over at Munny's house. In a bed.

Lester   That's a start.

Cory Remember I told you about the psychiatrist, Armand?

Lester Is he helping?

Cory I think so. He came back from Miami and brought me a nice present. And you'll never guess who his uncle turns out to be.

Lester Father Riordan.

Cory (*surprised*) How did you know?

Lester (*smiling*) Well . . .

Cory (*a penny drops*) What? You and Father Riordan fixed me up?

Lester *grins knowingly.*

Cory (*surprised*) You devil! I'd better go. He's waiting for me outside.

Lester Will you give me a kiss?

Cory (*pause*) Yes, Papa.

Lester Will you kiss me without washing your hands and face afterwards?

Cory (*pause*) I'll try, Papa.

She kisses him.

Good night.

Lester I'm sorry I didn't return your call when you were . . . y'know . . .

Cory . . . pregnant.

Lester I should have said 'come home'. Why didn't I say 'come home?'

Cory It's okay, Papa. It'll be okay.

She looks to the bathroom and physically forces herself to go to the door and she exits. The lights fade and up again to reveal **Monroe** *in* **Lester**'s *room. Again it is late at night.*

Monroe   Father, are you awake?

Lester   What? What is it? Who is it?

Monroe   It's me, Monroe.

Lester   Good Lord, Munny, what time is it?

Monroe   About ten thirty.

Lester   What day is it?

Monroe   Tomorrow is Thursday.

Lester   Time is passing so fast.

Monroe   Listen, Father, Cory and I – we're worried about Ike. He's a little crazy you know. We've looked all over town and we can't find him. We're concerned he might do something.

Lester   What something?

Monroe   About the wedding. We don't know. Just be careful. Okay?

Lester   I'm always careful. Say, did I ever tell you when I was in the Navy they called me Prunzie?

Monroe   (*brusque*)   No you didn't. Listen, Father, I have got to ask you one last time not to marry this girl. We cannot respect it.

Lester   You want me to be lonely in my old age?

Monroe   Of course not. You just can't marry her. Be her friend, her partner.

Lester   Munny. Let me tell you something. I named you after a great president.

Monroe   You never told me. But James Monroe wasn't great.

Lester   At least he had a doctrine. *He* had principles.

Monroe   So do I.

Lester (*confrontational*)   I don't think so. When you were a kid you were my favorite. When you graduated third in your class I wanted to tell you I was proud, but you were so self-centered the words stuck in my throat. You never paid any attention to your mother or me except for what you could get out of us. What do you take me for? An idiot? A dumb TV repairman who doesn't know what's going through that devious mind of yours?

Monroe   You're not being fair to me or my boys, Father. They're your only grandchildren, for Christ sake.

Lester   Don't give me that! They're just as selfish as you are! I can't even remember which one is Bob and which one is Roger.

Monroe   I worked hard to gain your respect, Father. When I got my accounting degree you wouldn't even get me a job with your friend Peccorino.

Lester   How could I recommend you? I didn't trust you. And if you were working at Peccorino's you would have seen my books. You would have cheated me.

Monroe (*angry*)   How can you insult me like that? I don't cheat.

Lester (*loudly*)   You don't, eh? You chase after women which is why Louise divorced you. You cheated your own brother over your grandfather's silver dollars. If I made you executor you'd probably cheat him again. You're a cheater, Monroe, and you lie.

Monroe   Well, you lied to us about what you were worth!

Lester (*agitated*)   I never lied. I just never told you. Why should I tell you my secrets? I was awake when you used to sneak around in here, rummaging in my drawers looking for my papers. I kept quiet because I was too embarrassed to confront you. How could you be so underhanded, Monroe?

And how dare you badger Gil Peccorino about my books and threaten to take him to court? Did you think he wouldn't tell me?

Monroe (*demanding*)   I'm your eldest son! I'm entitled to know!

Lester (*louder*)   You're only entitled to know what I want you to know about my business! (*Pause, deep breaths, trying to be calmer.*) Look here, Munny. Your brother and sister looked up to you and you let them down. But it's not too late to make it up to them. I beg you to dig down and try to find some love inside your heart and figure out a way to share it with them. As the Japanese say, 'one kind word can warm three winter months'.

Monroe *walks slowly to the door. He turns.*

Monroe   You are going to cut us out of your will altogether, aren't you?

Lester   There will always be some things Munny can't buy.

Monroe   What's that supposed to mean?

Lester   It's not over 'til it's over.

Monroe   I'm sorry. I'll try harder to be what you wanted me to be.

Lester   That's a start. And I hear you've been helping your sister. Keep it up.

Monroe   I'd better go. Be careful, Father. Tell that nurse to be careful too.

Lester (*pause*)   Thanks . . . son.

The lights fade. Music cue: a Koto arpeggio. The lights fade up on **Lily** *wheeling in the tea tray on a trolley.*

Lily   The Japanese Tea Ceremony is an important part of our culture. We don't have the equipment to do it properly here at Bayside Manor, but we'll pretend. First I put the sayu or hot water into the chawan – tea bowl. Then you sip it ever so gently to make sure it is not too hot.

Lester I see.

She holds the bowl for him and he sips.

Lily Do you like the tea?

Lester It's okay, but I'd prefer gin with a little sake.

Lily Some bartenders call that a SakeTini.

Lester That's stupid. 'Kamikaze cocktail' sounds a lot better!

Lily (*beat*) Tell me something, Lester.

Lester Yes, Lily.

Lily That time when you were in the Navy?

Lester Yes.

Lily Were you punished for eating all those prunes?

Lester All I remember is that I couldn't leave the bathroom for two whole days. (*Beat.*) Our wedding will be a remarkable day, Lily.

Lily Yes, it will.

Lester Are you nervous?

Lily A little.

Lester You are my joy, my angel.

Lily I want to be everything you want me to be.

Lester I have never been good at saying thank you. You must know that I thank you for doing this. I thank you for your youth and your beauty, your culture, your heritage and your love.

Lily You don't have to say it. I know.

Lester I thank you for teaching me important things . . . helping me realize things.

Lily I'm glad.

Lester   It's normal for sick people to contemplate their mortality.

Lily   I know.

Lester   Your little boy likes me.

Lily   He thinks you are a very funny man.

Lester   He is the youngest person I know. Some day he will be the last.

Lily   How so?

Lester   When the last person who ever knew you dies, that's when you yourself are really dead. Your boy will be the last person to remember me. (*Pause.*) Lily?

Lily   Yes, Lester.

Lester   Have you seen Ike?

Lily   Not recently, no.

Lester   If you do, it's important that you let me know right away, okay?

Lily   I will. (*Pause.*) Lester?

Lester   Yes, Lily?

Lily   What does 'shnozola like Durante' mean?

Lester   Jimmy Durante was a great entertainer with a big shnozola . . . (*Pointing to his nose.*) . . . his nose. He called his late wife 'Mrs Calabash' and always said goodnight to her at the end of every show. 'Goodnight, Mrs Calabash . . .'

Lily   He must have loved her very much.

Lester   I think I need a little rest now.

Lily   Of course.

Lester   I liked the tea.

Lily (*snapping off his light*)   Doitashimashite.

Lester   What does that mean, Lily?

Lily   Sleep tight.

Lights snap up again revealing **Ike** *sitting on the chair next to* **Lester**'s *bed.* **Lester** *is asleep.* **Ike** *holds a large pillow and kneads it, tormented. He gets up, puts the pillow down on the chair, and goes into the bathroom. He starts to retch, but nothing comes up. He is distraught. He goes back to the chair and clutches the pillow. He goes to the bed and hovers over his father. He's not going to . . . !*

Lester   Who's there?

Ike   It's me, Pop.

Lester   Ikey? You scared me. I thought it was the grim reaper. What time is it?

Ike   It's about one in the morning. Here's a pillow. I'll put it behind your head.

He does so.

Lester   What day is it?

Ike   Saturday.

Lester   It's my wedding day.

Ike   Yeah. Your wedding day.

Lester   Your brother and sister have been worried about you.

Ike   I just went up to the Beaverkill River for a few days to think.

Lester   Did you have a good think, at our old spot?

Ike   Yeah. I thought and thought. I remembered everything.

Lester   Did you remember punching out your brother Franklin?

Ike   Yeah. I beat myself up over that. He hugged me, Pop. I guess he's forgotten.

Lester   Maybe he's forgiven.

Ike   I would like that.

Lester   Did I ever tell you when I was in the Navy they called me Prunzie?

Ike   Why was that, Pop?

Lester   It's not important. What are you doing here so late?

Ike   I wanted to be alone with you. It's been a very long time since we were alone together.

Lester   It was in the car. The old Plymouth. I bailed you out and came to pick you up from the jail downtown.

Ike   I was only a kid. I was scared.

Lester   It was your first time. I was mad at you.

Ike   You kept asking me why I did it. You assumed I was guilty.

Lester   You were.

Ike   That's not the point, Pop. You didn't even want to hear my side of the story.

Lester   I raised you to be honest.

Ike   You didn't raise me, Pop. You were at the shop. I raised me.

Lester   I was a good father. I never laid a finger on you.

Ike   Maybe you should've.

Lester   You were always my favorite, Ikey. I named you after a great general.

Ike   Yeah, sure. Hey, guess who I ran into the other day?

Lester   Who?

Ike   The Don. Ettore Santangelo.

Lester   Where?

Ike (*lying*)   Um, at a club.

Lester   Really, Ikey? I know he never leaves his house.

Ike   He told me about you.

Lester   Oh?

Ike   He told me what a big deal you were. He told me about that Super Bowl game.

Lester   That was something.

Ike   They gave you a trophy. You never told me.

Lester (*choked laugh*)   Your mother hated it.

Ike   Why?

Lester   The inscription read 'To the Best Screwer in Town'!

Ike   That's funny. He also told me how much business the mob threw your way after the game. He told me about the Zenith Fund.

Lester   It's true.

Ike   We were rich, Pop. Why didn't we know it?

Lester   I never knew any kid with lots of dough who was happy, Ike. They spent it on drugs and nightclubs.

Ike   Yeah, yeah. Fast cars and fancy women. If you gave me money maybe I wouldn't have needed my schemes.

Lester   And now? You still have schemes?

Ike   No more. Inside I took a course on fixing computers. The instructor said I was a natural, Pop, and you know what I said?

Lester   What?

Ike   I told him my old man was the best TV repairman on Long Island. I could be the best computer fixer. I learned how to write code. You did Morse Code. I can do C plus plus. I'm just like you, Pop.

Lester   You are?

Ike   Guess where I'm working.

Lester   I can't.

Ike (*embarrassed to admit*)   There's a computer store on East Main, five stores away from where your old shop was. I'm in the back room, Pop. I'm wearing a brown smock just like you used to wear. And first thing every morning I open a bag of oily sawdust and toss it on the floor like kitty litter, and then I sweep it up.

Lester   Does Munny know? Does Cory?

Ike   No, Pop.

Lester   Do you think it's beneath you, being a common repairman . . . like me?

Ike   I wanted to be a wise guy, not some two-bit screwdriver jockey hanging around the wholesale house. I wanted to pull off a big score. Ain't that funny? You got rich being honest. Who would have thought?

Lester   I never thought I'd say it, but I'm proud of you, Ikey. From now on it's going to be different.

Ike   How can it be different? You're getting married in a few hours. You're going to give your fortune to her.

Lester   Have I ever lied to you?

Ike   How should I know? You never told me nothing!

Lester   I'll tell you something now. Everything's going to be alright. You'll see. Now go home and get some sleep.

Ike   Okay, Pop.

He gets up to go.

Lester   And Ikey.

Ike   Yeah, Pop.

Lester   Stop calling your brother a prick to his face!

Ike *exits. The lights dim.* **Helen***'s urn light comes on and she materializes, sitting in a chair next to* **Lester***'s bed.*

Helen   Who would've thought that he's the one most like you?

Lester   I wasn't a thief.

Helen   Maybe it was a cry for attention. (*Pause.*) So today's the big day.

Lester   Yes. I've had some pain in my legs. The doctors say I shouldn't be moved, so the wedding will take place here.

Helen   In this room?

Lester   Yes.

Helen   Don't forget to take off your wedding ring for the ceremony.

Lester   Domo for reminding me.

Helen   It won't be like our wedding.

Lester   No, you won't be there.

Helen *rises. She begins to dance as if she is dancing with him.*

Helen   Do you remember our wedding waltz?

Lester   We swept across the floor like Fred Astaire and Ginger Rogers.

Helen   Everyone applauded.

Lester   Even your father who hated me.

Helen   The world was our oyster.

She glides and turns, faster and faster.

Lester   I was the proudest man in New York.

Helen   We were so in love.

Lester   So carefree at twenty-three.

She spins round and round and evaporates into blackness. A few seconds later the lights fade back up revealing the wedding party gathered around **Lester** *who wears a black bow tie.* **Ike** *is in a sport coat and jeans and* **Cory** *in a lovely dress.* **Monroe** *joins them.* **Lily**, *in demure bridal outfit carrying a corsage, stands on* **Lester**'s *right. Best man* **Barry Gillis** *stands on his left.* **Father Riordan** *officiates.* **Helen**'s *urn has been removed from its stand.*

Lester   Well, it's time. The papers have been signed. The doctors have given their okay. Let's get this show on the road. (*To* **Lily**.) Are you ready, my little geisha girl?

Lily   I'm ready, my big samurai.

Lester   Father Riordan. Bonzai!

Father Riordan   Dearly beloved and honored guests: We are gathered together here this day in the sight of God, and company assembled, to join this man and this woman in holy matrimony, an honorable estate instituted by God and blessed by Christ. If any man can show just cause why Lester and Lily may not lawfully be joined together, let him now speak, or else hereafter forever hold his peace.

There is a long pause. **Cory**, **Monroe** *and* **Ike** *look at each other wishing they could say something, but knowing they cannot. Finally:*

Father Riordan   Do you, Lester, take Lily . . .

Lester   I object.

Ike   *You* can't object, Pop, you're the fuckin' groom!

Lester   I can't let Lily go through with it.

Ike   Yes you can. We've come to terms with it.

Cory   What is it, Papa, are you ill?

Lester   No. There's a good reason why Lily can't marry me.

Cory   What is it?

Lester   She's already married!

A stunned pause.

Everyone   She's what?! Married? What did he say? But I don't understand. How can she be . . . ?

Lester   She's too smart to be a bigamist.

Cory   But Father Riordan told me . . . Father Riordan? What's going on here?

Father Riordan   Corinne, I cannot tell a lie. I told you a lie. But I think the good Lord will forgive me for it. Lily is not a widow. Her husband just got back from Japan.

Ike *and* **Monroe**   Her husband?! You're joking!

Lester   And I told a bigger lie.

Cory   What was that, Papa?

Lester   I said that I was in love with Lily. I do love her in a special way, but the only woman I ever really loved was your mother.

Cory   This is insane!

Lily   And I lied too.

Cory   How did you lie?

Lily   I'm not Catholic.

Ike   I knew it.

Lily   I'm Jewish.

Cory   That's impossible!

Lily (*to* **Cory**, *friendly conversationally*)   No, it's true. There is a big synagogue in Kobe. We are descended from the lost tribes of Israel.

Barry (*confused*)   Does this mean the wedding is off? I'm not the big enchilada anymore?

Father Riordan (*quickly, fluently*)   Usted no es el padrino de la boda falsa de hoy, señor Barry!

Barry   Do I know what that means? Wait! What about the ring?

Lester   It's paste, Barry. Just paste.

Fast fade. A light fades up on **Monroe** *downstage left. He addresses the audience as he did in his mother's memorial at the start.*

Monroe   Those of you who were there won't forget the most amazing wedding feast Father arranged. Everyone at Bayside Manor was invited. Lily's husband had brought some weird fish all the way from Japan. A band had been hired and their adorable little boy danced with some of the old ladies. At about one o'clock Father was nodding off so we all went home.

Lights fade on **Monroe** *and up on* **Lester***'s bed. There is no light on the urn.* **Helen** *stands off to the side in half-light. She doesn't move, her face impassive. From underneath the covers we hear a giggle, and another.* **Lester** *lifts his head and lets out with an enormous belly laugh. He does not rise from his bed.*

Lester   Helen, are you there? I did it. I really pulled it off. (*Pause.*) Did you see it? Did you see the expressions on their faces? And what a party! My lips are still tingling from the fuku. Where are you, Helen? Oh my darling, I think it worked. I think I closed the circle and Franklin will be alright at last. Can you hear me, Helen? Listen: I've come to my senses. I can say it now. I was a rotten father. I was inflexible, intolerant, cheap. Lily showed me how fathers in Japan work with their children to develop trust. They must even pass a test. I never did that. I blamed them for everything, but it was me. It was my fault. I hope they will forgive me . . . I really think – they're starting to like me. Maybe one day they will forget . . . even love . . . Helen, are you listening? Why can't I see you? You've always been here when I needed you. And I need you now, because today is one of the happiest days of my life.

Helen *stands impassively, sadly, perhaps tearfully as the lights fade. The lights come up on* **Monroe** *downstage continuing to address the audience.*

Monroe (*choking up*)   The next morning, the morning after his pretend wedding, father didn't wake up. Another monumental stroke of luck. Bad luck.

Scene Six

The lights come up on **Barry Gillis**'s *living room as in Act One, Scene One. Now there are two urns on the mantelpiece.* **Cory**, **Ike**, **Barry** *and* **Father Riordan** *are gathered, as is* **Lily**. *They address the audience directly as it is a memorial service for* **Lester**.

Monroe (*to audience*)   Two weeks after his funeral, we were summoned to the offices of Bobrow Haas and Partners in Astoria for the reading of the will.

Cory   There were more people than I expected and I was surprised to see some Italian men who used to live in the old neighborhood – Indelicato, Calabrase . . . Santangelo.

Ike   Old man Bobrow got up and started reading the bequests. I couldn't believe it! Pop gave money to a Brazillian library to replace books eaten by termites. And he had bought ten acres of plum trees in California for Lily's kid.

Monroe   He left funds to protect some endangered wildcat species in Madagascar! Why?

Cory   And of course he gave big grants to Bayside Manor and for a memorial wing in Mother's name at the home.

Father Riordan   And everyone is invited to see the new
Lester Riley recreation room at St Hughs when it opens in
June.

Cory   He also left money for Lily to go to medical school.

Lily   Lester wanted to find a way to bring his children
together, but he could not. I told him 'Nanakorobi Yaoki' –
'If you fall seven times, rise eight times'. He said, 'You are so
smart I should marry you, my little geisha girl'. And the
charade was born. (*Wide-eyed with admiration.*) But I never
realized until he died . . . that Lester had such a great
shnozola for business.

Barry   Muy grande. He even gave me a trip to Mexico City
and a total Spanish immersion course at Berlitz!

Monroe   I added up Father's legacy in my head and it
reached the two point three mil he had at Morgan Stanley.

Cory   Then Mr Bobrow said, 'The administrators of the
Zenith Investment Fund gathered here today are instructed
to pay all monthly dividends directly to my children. I
hereby appoint as executor my son (*Pause.*) Franklin. He will
countersign all transfers so you will need to visit him on the
first of every month. You know how much Franklin likes to
sign his name.'

Ike   You wouldn't believe how much money was in that
fund!

Monroe   And then Bobrow takes out a stack of airline
tickets from Westerman Travel for the three of us, my boys,
and for Cory's new boyfriend, Armand. Father had arranged
the whole thing – Paris, Rome, London, and even the
pyramids in Egypt.

Cory   He must've been planning it for months.

Ike   We're leaving next week.

Monroe   Y'know a strange thing happened this morning. I
went to the mailbox and inside was a hundred silver dollars
that were stolen in a burglary some years back. Weird, eh?

Ike (*with a knowing smile*)   Freaky.

Monroe (*to* **Ike**)   And you know what I'm going to do with them?

Ike   What's that, Foss . . . uh, Munny?

Monroe   We'll have poker nights at my house and use them as chips.

Cory (*wringing her hands in gleeful anticipation*)   Deal *me* in.

Monroe (*to audience*)   Several of you have asked to speak today to remember our father. First up is Barry Gillis.

Barry   I'll keep this short and sweet. I just want to say 'gracias' to you all for coming to my home for the last time. I sold it, and mañana I'm moving to an apartment at Bayside Manor – on the third floor. (*Smiles.*) I'm told there's a Mrs Gomez there who speaks excellent Español and dances flamenco caliente! Now let me tell you a few things about Lester Riley. When the chips were down he was a real stand-up guy who never muddied the waters . . .

The lights fade down until there are only two spots on the brass urns on the mantelpiece. **Lester**'s *bed appears. He and* **Helen** *lie side by side in the bed.*

Helen   You did real good, Lester.

Lester   They are finally talking to each other.

Helen   They might even be friends one day.

Lester   I gave them something to fight against – me!

Helen   Everybody wins.

Lester   Even Franklin.

Helen   They were all together at your cremation. Even Munny's boys.

Lester   I'll tell you something I've learned, Helen: All men are cremated equal.

Helen   Very clever, dopey doo.

Lester   Oyasumi, Helen.

Helen   Good night . . . Prunzie.

Lester (*Durante impression*)   And good night Mrs Calabash wherever you are.

Music in: Jimmy Durante singing 'Make Someone Happy'.

Curtain.

The End.

Bloomsbury Methuen Drama Modern Plays

include work by

Bola Agbaje
Edward Albee
Davey Anderson
Jean Anouilh
John Arden
Peter Barnes
Sebastian Barry
Alistair Beaton
Brendan Behan
Edward Bond
William Boyd
Bertolt Brecht
Howard Brenton
Amelia Bullmore
Anthony Burgess
Leo Butler
Jim Cartwright
Lolita Chakrabarti
Caryl Churchill
Lucinda Coxon
Curious Directive
Nick Darke
Shelagh Delaney
Ishy Din
Claire Dowie
David Edgar
David Eldridge
Dario Fo
Michael Frayn
John Godber
Paul Godfrey
James Graham
David Greig
John Guare
Mark Haddon
Peter Handke
David Harrower
Jonathan Harvey
Iain Heggie

Robert Holman
Caroline Horton
Terry Johnson
Sarah Kane
Barrie Keeffe
Doug Lucie
Anders Lustgarten
David Mamet
Patrick Marber
Martin McDonagh
Arthur Miller
D. C. Moore
Tom Murphy
Phyllis Nagy
Anthony Neilson
Peter Nichols
Joe Orton
Joe Penhall
Luigi Pirandello
Stephen Poliakoff
Lucy Prebble
Peter Quilter
Mark Ravenhill
Philip Ridley
Willy Russell
Jean-Paul Sartre
Sam Shepard
Martin Sherman
Wole Soyinka
Simon Stephens
Peter Straughan
Kate Tempest
Theatre Workshop
Judy Upton
Timberlake Wertenbaker
Roy Williams
Snoo Wilson
Frances Ya-Chu Cowhig
Benjamin Zephaniah

Bloomsbury Methuen Drama Contemporary Dramatists

include

John Arden (two volumes)
Arden & D'Arcy
Peter Barnes (three volumes)
Sebastian Barry
Mike Bartlett
Dermot Bolger
Edward Bond (eight volumes)
Howard Brenton (two volumes)
Leo Butler
Richard Cameron
Jim Cartwright
Caryl Churchill (two volumes)
Complicite
Sarah Daniels (two volumes)
Nick Darke
David Edgar (three volumes)
David Eldridge (two volumes)
Ben Elton
Per Olov Enquist
Dario Fo (two volumes)
Michael Frayn (four volumes)
John Godber (four volumes)
Paul Godfrey
James Graham
David Greig
John Guare
Lee Hall (two volumes)
Katori Hall
Peter Handke
Jonathan Harvey (two volumes)
Iain Heggie
Israel Horovitz
Declan Hughes
Terry Johnson (three volumes)
Sarah Kane
Barrie Keeffe
Bernard-Marie Koltès (two volumes)
Franz Xaver Kroetz
Kwame Kwei-Armah
David Lan
Bryony Lavery
Deborah Levy
Doug Lucie

David Mamet (four volumes)
Patrick Marber
Martin McDonagh
Duncan McLean
David Mercer (two volumes)
Anthony Minghella (two volumes)
Tom Murphy (six volumes)
Phyllis Nagy
Anthony Neilson (two volumes)
Peter Nichol (two volumes)
Philip Osment
Gary Owen
Louise Page
Stewart Parker (two volumes)
Joe Penhall (two volumes)
Stephen Poliakoff (three volumes)
David Rabe (two volumes)
Mark Ravenhill (three volumes)
Christina Reid
Philip Ridley (two volumes)
Willy Russell
Eric-Emmanuel Schmitt
Ntozake Shange
Sam Shepard (two volumes)
Martin Sherman (two volumes)
Christopher Shinn
Joshua Sobel
Wole Soyinka (two volumes)
Simon Stephens (three volumes)
Shelagh Stephenson
David Storey (three volumes)
C. P. Taylor
Sue Townsend
Judy Upton
Michel Vinaver (two volumes)
Arnold Wesker (two volumes)
Peter Whelan
Michael Wilcox
Roy Williams (four volumes)
David Williamson
Snoo Wilson (two volumes)
David Wood (two volumes)
Victoria Wood

For a complete catalogue
of Bloomsbury Methuen Drama
titles write to:

Bloomsbury Methuen Drama
Bloomsbury Publishing Plc
50 Bedford Square
London WC1B 3DP

or you can visit our website at:
www.bloomsbury.com/drama